# THE
# SHAKESPEARE
# AND COMPANY
# BOOK OF
# INTERVIEWS

# THE SHAKESPEARE AND COMPANY BOOK OF INTERVIEWS

INTRODUCED BY SYLVIA WHITMAN
EDITED BY ADAM BILES

CANONGATE

First published in Great Britain, the USA and Canada in 2023
by Canongate Books Ltd, 14 High Street, Edinburgh EH1 1TE

Distributed in the USA by Publishers Group West
and in Canada by Publishers Group Canada

canongate.co.uk

1

*British Library Cataloguing-in-Publication Data*
A catalogue record for this book is available on
request from the British Library

ISBN 978 1 80530 003 8

Typeset in Bembo by Palimpsest Book Production Ltd,
Falkirk, Stirlingshire

Printed and bound in Great Britain by Clays Ltd, Elcograf S.p.A.

To independent booksellers everywhere

# Contents

~

# Introduction

## By Sylvia Whitman

~

When my father, George Whitman, opened the doors to this book-shop in 1951, it was just three narrow ground-floor rooms – arranged in a line like train carriages – with no electricity, and with George's bed wedged in between the shelves. Despite the lack of space, George immediately started hosting free seminars, workshops for artists and writers and informal discussions. He considered these 'an evening school for those who regard education as a permanent life process'. For George – as for booksellers across the globe – ordering and unpacking books, finding titles to sell or lend to curious readers, and hosting events were all part of the same continuum.

By the middle of the decade, the bookshop had expanded to include the first-floor flat, and had become a gathering place for Paris-based writers including Anaïs Nin, Julio Cortázar and Richard Wright, many of whom George persuaded to read from their work, or sign their books at public gatherings. Indeed, a single issue of George's broadside, *Paris Book News* from Winter 1956 announces a signing by James Baldwin; Christmas carol singing; a dialogue on Modern French Poetry; a selection of lectures (including the very intriguing *Cybernetics and the Arts* by 'poet and statistician' Charles Hatcher); a 'Cycle of Folksongs'; and a reception for Wright.

# Introduction

The bookshop had also become known as a free place to crash in exchange for helping out. George called these guests 'Tumbleweeds'. Their constant presence at Shakespeare and Company then, and in the decades since, meant that even when the bookshop closed its doors for the night, the discussion of books continued.

By April 1958, the Beats had come to Paris. Allen Ginsberg agreed to read from *Howl*, alongside other poets including Gregory Corso. In front of a crowd that spilled onto the terrace, Corso got naked. Never one to be upstaged, Ginsberg followed suit. Later, William Burroughs spontaneously gave one of the first public – and fully-clothed – readings from the work-in-progress that would become *Naked Lunch*. George later remarked that 'nobody was sure what to make of it, whether to laugh or be sick'.

Even when the bookshop was temporarily closed between 1966 and 1968 as part of the French government's 'Operation Anti Beatnik', readings, lectures and discussions continued under the guise of what George baptised the Free University of Paris.

By the early 1980s, the bookshop had grown in size and reputation, and often felt like one constant event. This feeling was fuelled by people like the wonderful Ted Joans – Beat poet, and one of my first friends – who would come by at noon every day to read *The International Herald Tribune*, and to recite his poetry in front of the bookshop to anyone who stopped to listen. I was fortunate to begin my life in this centuries-old building in the heart of Paris that was at once a library, performance space and shop – albeit one selling 'products' that are not really products at all, but life-changing entities, magical containers of universes that can be slipped inside your jacket pocket.

This 'lovely combination, this solitude and gathering', as Lewis Buzbee so eloquently describes independent bookstores in *The Yellow-Lighted Bookshop*, stayed with me. When I returned to live at the bookshop in my twenties, events had taken the form of the '*lundi littéraire*', an oh-so disorganised but utterly charming weekly gathering. Every Monday a poster was tacked onto the front window, often just with the name of that week's guest – sometimes scribbled on the back of a bill, sometimes by the author themselves – and the words: *Event! Tonight! 7pm! All Welcome!*

Around this time, four friends and I organised a literary festival in the park next door. I thought I could put on an event in the shadow of the bookshop but not have it taken over by my father. When I tentatively showed him the programme his response was immediate, very loud and characteristically pragmatic: 'But who is going to cook for all these writers?!' Beneath the eccentricity of this exclamation lies something that George understood very well, and that my partner David Delannet and I try to keep alive today: if we are the hosts of a literary event, that means writers and readers alike are our guests.

Giving a bed to writers has long been key to our identity, not just young 'Tumbleweeds' who sleep between our shelves, but also the more established authors who come to stay in our writer's flat. Having these guests wander downstairs to read from their work, to people who can then take those very words home with them in a book, feels like an organic way of discovering a work of art. After a couple of years when visiting writers have been thin on the ground, and events few and far between, David and I have truly come to appreciate the magic of having the creator of a work present in the bookshop.

But let's not over-romanticise here. Not every event is idyllic. There's the book which crashes down from the shelf, just missing the surprised author's head. There's the awkward silence when nobody in the audience comes forth with a question. There are also those moments when the writer gets transported by the creative spirit and gives what to them feels like a 'timeless' reading, but to the increasingly achy bottoms of the audience instead starts to feel like an eternity. I remember George dealing with moments like these by barging in, scooping up a candle, putting the flame to his hair and just letting it burn. This invariably led to shocked gasps from the audience and the reading quickly coming to a close. (If they'd known that this was just how George usually trimmed his hair, the effect might have been a little less dramatic.)

What is it that makes an event special? Is there a unique ingredient that unites Ted Joans's impromptu poetry readings, with an electrifying jazz performance, with the twenty extraordinary conversations you hold in your hand?

In the 1960s they weren't just known as 'events', but as 'happenings'. Literally that moment when something 'happens' – to the writer, to the audience, to the room itself. More specifically? It's a charge, a certain electricity. It's the convening of a group of people. The communion of those people. And the creation of something new from that communion. Or as Kae Tempest so perfectly puts it in *On Connection*, 'a story . . . must be engaged with to become powerful; the story must be read, the song must be listened to, in order to acquire its full charge . . . Connection is collaborative. For words to have meaning, they must be read.'

I think of each of the interviews in this book as its very own 'happening'. They are a selection of some of the most insightful conversations that have taken place within our walls, led by our very own Adam Biles, who has curated and developed these events over the past seven years. I have marvelled at his ability to engage in such intimate and profound conversations with some of the world's most interesting minds. I think in part this is because, as a writer himself, he shows a deep respect and sensitivity to the process, and agonies, of writing a book.

And while it's undoubtedly true that the ephemeral nature of 'happenings' contributes to what makes them special ('You really had to be there!') I do feel fortunate that, unlike most of the events in our bookshop's history, we had these ones recorded and can share some of that magic with you.

Now that events are more regular again, I realise how much we've missed them and what a unique thing they are. Just by owning this book, you are helping those events continue into the future, as all money raised from it will go to Friends of Shakespeare and Company, the non-profit we set up in 2020 to safeguard our non-commercial activities: our free events, open to all, but also our writer's residency and upstairs reading room, a space George said he wanted guests to enter like they had inherited a book-lined apartment on the Seine, all the more delightful because you shared it with others. I deeply believe in the importance of defending free communal spaces – not just bookshops, but libraries, parks and other such places.

Rereading these conversations, and thinking about Shakespeare and Company's history through the lens of its events, has left me with much to reflect upon, and with many unanswered questions about how future events might and should look in our rapidly changing world. As inspiration for that reflection – a communal one, I hope – I'd like to leave you with some words spoken by publisher and poet John Freeman during one of the many events he has chaired for us. John's words beautifully encapsulate how I feel not just about our bookshop, but about all indie bookshops and the vital role they will hopefully always play in bringing people together:

This is a beautiful space. There's a sound in the room when I'm not speaking. There's a vibration that happens when people are in the same space together. We feel that when we enter a space that's to some degree collective and free and open. That's why we are drawn here. That's why people are here instead of at a co-working space looking at something online. We need that togetherness.

# Preface

### By Adam Biles

~

I've lost count of how many writers I've interviewed, but it's certainly in the hundreds. Almost all of these conversations have taken place at Shakespeare and Company – around the Renaissance-era wishing well in the fiction room, in the cosy upstairs reading library, or on the cobbled terrace with Notre-Dame looming over us . . . and sometimes drowning us out with her bells. I cannot overstate the profound effect that this enchanting space has on writer, audience and interviewer alike.

The choice of which interviews to include in this book was not an easy one. We probably could have selected twenty completely different events and ended up with an equally interesting collection. Much of it came down to identifying those moments when the magic of the bookshop, the rapport between writer and interviewer, and the anticipation of the audience worked their curious alchemy. They are also all conversations in which the guest rejected the comfort of the trusted anecdote and pre-scripted answer, in favour of the more precarious but exciting route of new thought. On such evenings, an irresistible energy can be felt rising in the room until – if we get very lucky – it reaches what I call 'escape velocity'; that heady moment when the formal interview breaks its bounds, and becomes something more: a conversation that matters. A conversation which will, perhaps, resonate in the lives of everyone involved long after they've left the bookshop.

Revisiting these conversations – both those included here and dozens of others – I was struck by how many common themes crop up. There are subjects that have attracted increasing interest over the past decade: questions of representation, of who has the right to tell certain stories, of the relevance of the novel as a form, of the emergence of 'auto-fiction' on the anglophone scene. There are also the more timeless questions, about how to tell a story, about getting into the minds of characters, about navigating writer's block. One of the greatest pleasures in seeing these interviews collected in this way has been identifying those serendipitous moments when writers seem to directly address each other, months apart: Annie Ernaux and Carlo Rovelli engaging on the nature and experience of time; Jesmyn Ward, Hari Kunzru and George Saunders reflecting on the role of ghosts in fiction; Rachel Cusk, Meena Kandasamy and Claire-Louise Bennett laying out the challenges and pitfalls of attempting to map a life onto the page. The list could go on.

On a personal level, I have found it both interesting and a little emotional to note how much my own concerns crept into these conversations – as a writer, as a reader and as a human being muddling his way through life. (Although I will leave it to the inquisitive reader to figure out what those concerns were.) More than anything, however, seeing these conversations collected here, I just feel immensely privileged to have had the opportunity to speak to such brilliant thinkers in such a beautiful bookshop. And I look forward to doing so for many years to come.

# The Interviews

# Percival Everett

## *I'm Not Sidney Poitier*

### Monday 12th November 2012

~

**Adam Biles:** *I'm Not Sidney Poitier*, Percival Everett's seventeenth novel, follows the turbulent life of the eponymous character as he navigates the cognitive dissonance American society experiences when confronted with a very rich Black man. I should clarify that the protagonist's name is not 'Sidney Poitier', but 'Not Sidney Poitier', that's to say 'Not' is his first name and, not, as you may have thought, and rightfully expected, an adverb. I hope that clears things up . . . *I'm Not Sidney Poitier* is a riotous picaresque, from a writer who understands that the best, perhaps only, way to treat subjects of the utmost gravity is through humour. Percival Everett, welcome to Shakespeare and Company.

The first thing I wanted to talk about is the idea of identity in your work – in *I'm Not Sidney Poitier*, but also in a novel like *Erasure* – where a flagging novelist finds renewed success after releasing a novel under a pseudonym. What is it about the ideas of characters being, or indeed not being, someone else that interests you?

**Percival Everett:** I think I'm more interested in the notion of my identity than identity itself. When I say that, I recognise immediately that every work of art is about identity of some kind. So even though I'm always either accused or reported as having an interest in identity, I'm not sure that it's something that's singular or particular to my work. Just sort of a necessary component of a work. That said, part of the reason I write is I love the beautiful arithmetic of things, and I'm always fascinated by that. By the property of identity. That $A$ equals $A$, which seems somehow wrong. Because one is on the left of the equals sign and the other is on the right.

**AB:** So in that equation, there's also almost a mirror image rather than an identity.

**PE:** Yeah. I mean, you know, when we look in the mirror, we're not seeing an identical representation of ourselves. We're seeing a mirror image. I suppose photographs are the closest thing, but even then we're seeing a photograph. I don't know what's in a photograph. It used to be silver and metal and stuff. Now we're seeing pixels.

**AB:** On that subject of reflection and representation, there are a couple of instances in your work when a character, a certain Percival Everett, appears. At the beginning of *I'm Not Sidney Poitier*, you state that he should not be confused with the writer. And yet, by giving a character your name you are surely setting the trap for the reader to make that confusion. How does Percival Everett the character serve Percival Everett the writer?

**PE:** I think I've only been a character in that one novel, thank goodness. I was having fun with a lot of different people and I thought, 'well, I might as well make fun of myself'. Turns out I'm very easy to make fun of. That was a little bit depressing. It actually comes out of this notion of non-fiction. It always strikes me as kind of bizarre that we should have a designation in which something is defined by what it is not. But that happens too in American culture. We have the term 'non-white'. That's why I grew up thinking, 'white people think I wake up and look in the mirror and say, "yeah, I'm not white".' So I just play with that.

**AB:** You certainly have a lot of fun with the Percival Everett character in that book. The reader is never sure if he's kind of a holy fool or just a fool . . .

**PE:** He's just a fool.

**AB:** OK, well that's settled . . . But like yourself, he's a teacher at the university. It's not that you give little value to university education, but you certainly satirise it, even mock the educational institutions, the literary theory and theorists. What makes them such ripe targets for satire?

**PE:** Well, because the stakes are so low. I teach literary theory as well as fiction writing. And what I essentially do is teach my graduate students to make fun of philosophers. I do that for two reasons: one is you can't really make fun of something unless you know it. And secondly, in making fun of it you often come to appreciate the thing that you're satirising. So even though I have myself on, and I'm making fun of the classroom and university, part of it is that I take that stuff very seriously.

**AB:** We do find a lot of references to philosophers in your work. In the extract you read [from *Percival Everett By Virgil Russell*] you mentioned Bertrand Russell and Wittgenstein, and you reference Schopenhauer in one of your other books. Is there a branch of philosophy that particularly interests you?

**PE:** No, everybody's fair game.

**AB:** For interest or for mockery?

**PE:** Oh, both. Both.

**AB:** So on the subject of fair game for humour. In the books of yours I've read, humour is such a prominent strand. In *Sidney Poitier* it's very dominant, in others less so, but it's always there. When you conceive a book do you have a sense that it's going to be funny? Or is it the story that comes first and the humour that comes later?

**PE:** You know, I sit down with blank pages. That any words at all get put on them is kind of magical. I don't really know how that happens. I mean, where do novels come from? I had no idea. I hadn't thought about Sidney Poitier in twenty years. Then he called me and told me I owed him $50. First, I see a shape of a book. I see a logic in it. Then I come up with things in the world that bother me, and then I encode it in some way. So it makes some sense to me. Then I find a story that I can put on top of it. Then I get really bored with that story and I have to do something else to make it interesting to me. But with this novel *I'm Not Sidney Poitier* I can't tell you how it started . . .

Oh wait, actually I just remembered how it started. There was this awful television show in the US, I don't even know if it's still on. It's called *Maury* or something. It's where they take really poor people, and they come on the stage and they have all these fights and they do paternity tests. I was sitting at my desk one day and the television was on, and there was an ad for this show. They started saying, 'I am not, not, not, not, not, not, not, not, not, not, not the father'. And I heard the 'nots'. That was the beginning of *I Am Not Sidney Poitier*. That's what came to mind. I still didn't watch the show, though.

**AB:** It has the feel of an allegory, but at the same time there's not really a feeling of lessons learned or morals imparted by the end. Now, you've also worked with Greek myths in several of your works. What is it that interests you about these kind of forms?

**PE:** Well, there might be a moral, but I'm a writer and if you're looking to me for some kind of moral truth you're looking in the wrong place. I decided to spend my life trying to write stories and novels, and that's evidence enough that I'm morally deficient. So you shouldn't trust anything I say about anything.

I think anytime any artist starts out thinking that she or he knows an answer to something the work suffers. I think I have good questions, and I know I have my own political beliefs and my own moral beliefs, and nothing I can do is going to stop those things from filtering into the work. But the last thing I need to do is to think I have any message for anyone.

**AB:** I guess that the Greek myths are not really stories with morals. In fact, to modern eyes they can seem very morally ambiguous.

**PE:** I don't know how the myths were actually used. I've read lots about them, but I'm sure that part of the beauty of them in their early telling was that the gods are showing human frailty. The stories about the gods tell us about ourselves. They're pretty smart stories.

**AB:** Which kind of brings us back to this idea of reflection. Do you hope to reflect something about your reader back at them?

**PE:** I don't know. Most of the time I just hope that when I'm driving down the freeway the other driver stays on his side of the road. That's the only thing I've ever really worried about. But, you know, I did write a novel about Medea because I didn't like the story. Even when I was a kid there was something weird about it. Then as I got older, and I was a writer, it came back to me: Medea kills her children. And the reason she does it? She's crazy – but that's not good enough. So I wrote a novel to give Medea another chance.

**AB:** Connected to the subject of gods and myths: you've written an introduction to the Jefferson Bible, or a version of it. I've been trying to get hold of a copy without success. I'm just fascinated because it says on the marketing blurb for the book that you offered an atheist's eye view on the Jefferson Bible. Would you be able to tell us a little bit about what you wrote in the introduction?

**PE:** Oh God. If I could remember! I know there's a brief dialogue between Jefferson and myself. My grandfather was an atheist and my father was an agnostic. I am what I call an A-path. I simply don't care whether there's a guy up there.

**AB:** It's interesting then to accept such a commission.

**PE:** Well, there's the obvious problem of the author of the Declaration of Independence being a slave owner, and that's really what drew me to it. But also Jefferson, that notwithstanding, was a very smart man. And he was an agnostic. In the Bible that he composed he took the parts that he wanted to save. That was what was interesting to me. It's like someone who joins a club and then throws out all of the rules and employs their own. You get agnostics who believe that the teachings of Jesus are good teachings, but don't accept that he was the son of God. In fact some might even say that Jefferson would now have argued that there was no God. He just approved of the teachings of this man Jesus. So the character of Jefferson is fascinating to me.

**AB:** On the back of my copy of *Erasure* there's a quote from the *London Review of Books*, which describes you as 'America's pre-eminent post-racial novelist'. What do you think they mean by this term?

**PE:** I have no idea. It seems to me that to use the term 'post-racial' immediately invalidates your idea. If that were the case it would never occur to you to say 'post-racial'. So I don't know what that means.

**AB:** There often seems to be this attempt to classify writers by either a perceived style or something about their background. One word which I've seen repeatedly used to describe you is 'experimental'. Could you talk a little bit about your interest in the mechanics of the novel, in its form, and if you would accept the label of experimental?

**PE:** I used to give this lecture all over the place about there being no such thing as an experimental novel. My argument being that if you're writing a novel you have no idea what you're doing when you start, so you're reinventing the process and the form every time. In that way, every novel is experimental except for the most ground-out genre stuff. Then I wrote a novel called *The Water Cure*, and I thought maybe I have to shut up because it was such a strange novel. Now I look back at it and I realise that, no, it's just like all the other novels. There's a story. So it looks different? Big deal. I love abstract paintings and I used to avoid the term abstract. I used to say non-representational because I thought abstract sounded like there was no substance. Now I believe in the word abstract. What I want to make is an abstract novel. The problem with this is the medium that I use is representative by nature. It's very difficult to make an abstract thing out of representative elements.

Now my thinking, and I don't know if I succeed – and maybe

I will never succeed, but it keeps me writing – is can I make a novel that appears real that is abstract? I talk about nonsense a lot. I love nonsense. Especially Victorian nonsense, you know, Lewis Carroll and all that stuff. It's great stuff. And I load my novels with nonsense. Some people might say it's all nonsense. Nonsense is interesting because you have to adhere more firmly, more rigidly to a pattern than you would if you were saying anything else. Because the trick is, the words that don't make sense trick you into thinking that they do make sense. What does make sense to you is the rhythm, the structure and all that. So what I want to do is to write nonsense that actually makes sense. Wish me luck.

**AB:** I can feel the influence of books like *Tristram Shandy*, like *Don Quixote*, in your work. Does that ring true?

**PE:** Well, these are two that would be considered experimental novelists. Cervantes is writing a comment on the novels of chivalry. It was a real departure. And, again, humour plays an important part in that.

Even now there's no more post-modern text than *Tristram Shandy*. Even now. And I don't even think there's such a thing as post-modern. That's how post-modern *Tristram Shandy* is. There's that marbled page in that book, and when I saw that it was freeing. Why is that there? There's no reason why it's there. It's there, it's mad, and yet it fits. And it's beautiful. The beauty of the digression. You never get to the story that's announced to you. How beautiful is that? It's just, 'I'm gonna tell you my story', and they never get to it. That's just genius.

But it's not just writers. Recently I've given a couple of lectures on Antonioni. I remember the first time I saw *L'eclisse* was when I was sixteen. My father and I went to the arthouse in our town to see *L'eclisse* and it's got some weird racial stuff there that my father and I talked about. But I was sitting there watching this film and, again, I wasn't a writer yet, but there was no story. We're just moving through. As a kid, I played music, and I have to say, coming out of that film I realised I understood how to play jazz, because I wasn't boxed in any more.

I like to read nearly everything. Even stuff that I don't like, often the stuff I don't like, tells me more about writing novels than the stuff I do like. Not just what I don't want to do but sometimes things that I do want to do.

I always love a failed mess better than a safe success.

**AB:** You are remarkably prolific, or it seems so to me anyway. You've got seventeen novels now, short fiction, books of poetry . . .

**PE:** Let's get something straight: I'm not a poet. I write poems to prove that I can't write poetry, and I'm doing a pretty good job of it. I think most people agree with me.

**AB:** Even so, is it down to discipline?

**PE:** If I had to write with a schedule I'd shoot myself. I work when I feel like it. This could be from ranching for so long. At 5.30, I get up and feed the horses and then I have stuff to do all day long. I have ten, fifteen minutes here or there, and I don't have to get ready to work. That has stayed with me. So when I sit down, I'm working. I don't go on the internet at all. I check email, but it's like a bad neighbourhood I don't want to go into.

I had a friend who you always wondered why he wasn't getting any work done because he spent the first three hours of his four-hour work period looking at the internet. But he was the most extreme case I had ever seen. We were colleagues at a university. I saw his desk, which was very neat. Now I don't trust anyone with a neat desk. There's just something wrong if you have a neat desk – you know, he had all of his pencils in place. Then I was at his house for a lunch or something and I wandered into his study and there was this desk and it was an exact replica of his desk at school, the pencils and everything. I immediately became afraid of him.

So I don't worry. I don't get stressed out about anything. I know that's important. I know from being around horses. You just can't feel stress. And I realise that this is something I think all the time, because I'm writing these stories and in every story this one line shows up and I have to get rid of it: 'It's not a good thing. It's not a bad thing. It's just a thing.'

# Olivia Laing

## *The Lonely City*

### Tuesday 14th June 2016

~

**Adam Biles:** What does it mean to be lonely? How does that differ from simply being alone? How is it that a city of twenty million people can be one of the loneliest places on earth? What, if anything, can art do to alleviate the suffering? Olivia Laing explores all these questions, drawing on her own experiences and the lives of certain artists to produce a moving and provocative account of a condition that, while increasingly common, remains frighteningly taboo.

*The Lonely City* is a book that thrives in the cracks between genres. It educates, it informs, it moves. I would say it makes the reader want to put it down so they can rush out and discover or rediscover the work of the artists it documents; except, once you've picked it up *The Lonely City* is kind of impossible to put down. Please join me in welcoming Olivia Laing to Shakespeare and Company.

**Olivia Laing:** I'm absolutely thrilled to be here. I think this is the most beautiful, magical bookshop I've ever been in. And I spend a great deal of my life in bookshops. I haven't been in Paris, embarrassingly, since I was seventeen. I'm quite a lot older than that now.

So it really is just a massive thrill to be here, and to see so many people as well. Beautiful.

**AB:** One of the things I really love about your work is that the way you tackle your subjects feels very organic. It always seems that you experience certain things, and then the books rise out of that. So could you begin by talking a little bit about the genesis of the book?

**OL:** It's true, they do very much arise organically. I was in New York. I was actually writing my last book, *The Trip to Echo Spring*, and I was having a very strange time. A relationship that I had a lot of hope about had ended while I was in England, and I'd decided to come to New York independently of that. I had an instinct about New York – as people do about all kinds of cities, as perhaps people here have about Paris – that it's a place where you can have a kind of community. In particular, a kind of artistic community. I was right about that instinct for New York. I did find that there, but it took much longer than I was expecting. I was living in sublets, so I was really drifting. I was in my mid-thirties, everyone around me in England was getting married, having children. Their lives were moving in these directions that mine wasn't. So it was very alien-ating. And I'd gone to New York with those feelings of alienation. So I was in a fairly bleak place. I was also writing a book about alcoholism. I grew up in an alcoholic family. So, you know, I was dealing with quite raw material and I was lonely. I was really lonely. It wasn't particularly pleasant. But at the same time a writer is always two people. They're the person and they're the artist. And the artist in me, the critic in me, was fascinated by the almost immediate awareness that this was a taboo state. Loneliness is a taboo state. It's hard to confess. There isn't a language for talking about it. People don't even investigate it because of this sort of strange wall around it. So, while I was personally deeply miserable, at the same time I was aware that I had stumbled across a topic that was very under-handled and shameful. That's catnip to me! I'm drawn to shameful subjects, I think.

I knew from very early on that if I was going to write a book about it, it wasn't going to be a memoir. I don't write memoirs. I'm not very interested in them. I like having a thread of my own story and my own investment in the subject. But what I wanted was to come at it from multiple angles, which is why I used this group of different artists, some of whom were deeply socially isolated, the sort of stereotype of the lonely person. But some, like Andy Warhol, who is a major figure in this book, are more social. And yet he allows me to explore this sort of loneliness that I certainly could never have experienced personally.

**AB:** You said there's not really a vocabulary for dealing with it. So when you set about writing a book about it, I guess you have to try and come to some sort of broad definition of what loneliness is, to understand how it can be felt by somebody who's socially isolated, but also someone like Warhol. After writing the book have you come to a succinct definition?

**OL:** Yeah, and I suppose that comes partly from my own experience, and partly from reading so many different approaches. So the book has hard science in it. It has psychology in it. But when the first psychologists started writing about loneliness in the forties and fifties – you know, Freud never mentioned loneliness – they commented even then about how it is a subject that's talked about more in pop songs than almost anywhere else. And country songs!

I think a firm definition is quite simple. It is really not a lot to do with solitude. It's not necessarily about being physically isolated. You can be physically isolated and deeply, deeply content. You can live alone, never see anyone for months on end and be absolutely fine. On the other hand, you can be living in a city, you can have many friends, you can even be in a relationship – you can be married – and yet you can feel deeply lonely. And the reason for that is that loneliness is really about a longing for more intimacy than you have. It's not about just friendship, just the population of people in your life. It's about a deep level of feeling that you're loved, understood and in communication.

But I'd like to say something else about the language of it. In terms of trying to convey the experience, for me it was so visual talking about the art of loneliness. So much came up over and over, both in my own experience and in other peoples', of glass and ice as these two sort of metaphorical conveyors of this experience. That's about, on the one hand, being separated, and on the other hand feeling shamefully exposed. And I think that's why glass and ice, both of which are transparent, are the key symbols.

**AB:** It's fascinating that psychology and psychiatry didn't deal with it for so long. You write about it as being both shameful and alarming. That struck me as strange, for an emotion to be at once shameful and alarming, particularly since people don't necessarily think loneliness is something you bring on yourself. Why do you think there is this shame associated with loneliness?

**OL:** I think there's been a huge amount of work done over the last couple of decades about things like depression and anxiety. People have really, really worked hard to smash down the taboos around that, to make it more discussable in public. Loneliness has been weirdly resistant to that process. I think that's because it goes so deep in terms of what we are as humans. We are supposedly social creatures. We set great store in love, friendship and particularly romantic love. So I think it's immediately very, very tightly bound up with senses of social failure. It's very, very hard to admit that.

**AB:** I'd like to come on to talk about the artists now. We could probably spend at least an hour speaking about each of them individually, but I'd just like to pick up on a few different things. So the first one you deal with is Hopper. I think it's a choice that will resonate with a lot of people because, of course, *Nighthawks at the Diner* is one of the most well-known paintings in the world. But I, for one, knew very little about the man himself. And his is quite a surprising story.

**OL:** This happens all the time. If you're a writer who works in biographies, you discover that the people you're writing about aren't very nice. Not always. Sometimes they're wonderful. But with Hopper that did happen a little, in that I was very interested in the way that he'd communicated to me incredibly artfully this experience of entrapment, exposure, those very painful feelings. He sets up these scenarios in which people are separated from each other by architectural means, by walls, by windows. He makes spaces of intense division and longing. This is what's so magical about his work, what's so powerful about his work. And I wanted to get to grips with where that came from. Of course, biographical reasons aren't solely why anybody makes the art that they make, but I was interested in the biography because I didn't know a great deal about it. One of the things that I came across in Gail Levin's superb biography, *Edward Hopper: An Intimate Biography*, was his relationship with his wife. He married in his forties. He married late. She was also in her forties. She was also an artist. Her name's Jo Hopper. I'm guessing that absolutely no one in this room has ever seen any work by her. And the reason is that when she died, a few years after Hopper died, she left both their work to the Whitney Museum as his will decreed. And obviously you've all seen Hopper's work because the Whitney Museum took very good care of it, but they destroyed every one of her paintings. Part of what's so sad about that story is that Hopper also did everything he could to suppress her as an artist. Perhaps she was a terrible artist. It's totally possible.

But every woman in Hopper's paintings after they married is modelled by Jo. She's there: silent and stripped of her identity, stripped of her own agency. I haven't read her diaries. They're not available, but they are quoted at length in Gail's book. And she was desperate to make more art than she made and her husband stopped her. So that was a really dark story to come across.

**AB:** It's interesting, because it seems that it was a very close marriage nevertheless.

**OL:** They were very close. That's the other thing. They were very, very close. And if you watch any footage of the Hoppers being interviewed – and it's almost always the Hoppers – she's almost always there, and she speaks for him.

**AB:** You describe it as 'intimately adversarial'. Which is particularly interesting when coming back to the subject of loneliness, that you can have this intimate relationship . . .

**OL:** . . . and yet be lonely. It's such a lonely marriage. She says it's like waiting for the attention of an expensive watch specialist.

**AB:** There's a moment where he's talking about himself and he says, 'I probably am a lonely one'. That use of the indefinite article. He's not lonely. He is a lonely *one*. It's almost like loneliness is a deep part of his being.

**OL:** But it's also very democratic. His paintings are populated by lonely ones. I think part of why his paintings are so popular is that he gives you the sense of loneliness as something communal, and we forget that about loneliness when we're inside it. You feel like you're the only lonely person, and yet it's communal, which is really one of the threads of this book.

**AB:** And then there's Warhol, who seems on the surface a completely different character to Hopper, in his work, his art practice and also in his social life. One thing that struck me was how you say that before being lonely yourself you kind of dismissed Warhol's work. It didn't really speak to you.

**OL:** And I ended up loving him so much! I love Warhol. I love Warhol's work. I love the things that Warhol says about his work. I think he's such an interesting, weirdly underrated artist because he became so hyper-visible. And it was a video, actually; I spent a lot of time on YouTube during this period in New York, and I came across a video of him being interviewed. We think of Warhol as this sort of affectless, almost robotic figure wandering through the twentieth century. I was watching him being asked questions and struggling so hard to speak. He was blushing, he was stuttering. He was finding it very hard to get a sentence out. There was something of that agitated human body that made me very interested. I related to it at that moment, and it made me go back and look at his work and see it in a very different light. It's really about longing for, and terror of, intimacy. Things like the *Screen Tests*, things like the 'boring' movies of just watching somebody eat a sandwich or sleep. It's trying to get right up against the intimate, grainy experience of human life, and yet staying behind a camera to do so. That moved me so much.

**AB:** For my part, I'll admit, I didn't really have much of an opinion about him. I think he was one of those artists that you see so much of that you can barely see. But having read your book, certain things resonated so much more. That quotation, 'all the Cokes are the same and all the Cokes are good'. It's a Warholism. But when you see it in the context of someone who had deep difficulty engaging with other people and had this real sense of loneliness, suddenly there's a new poignancy to a lot of these things he said, and also to this quest to reproduce things in his work.

**OL:** He's a gay immigrant kid with poor health who feels different all the time. With those early screen prints of dollar bills and Campbell's soup cans he's reproducing American icons that the poor can possess, and he's reproducing them en masse. He wanted to call Pop Art 'Common Art'. It's this hugely democratic impulse that's about belonging. And I just find it moving.

**AB:** That connects to the work of an artist who takes a special place in the book, David Wojnarowicz. He's another gay artist, and the book explores sexuality quite a bit. Do you think there's something in that sense of difference, particularly, I guess, at the time that Warhol was growing up and Wojnarowicz was growing up, that almost inevitably led to loneliness, because they looked at society and they saw that they couldn't fit into the boxes prescribed for them?

**OL:** I think so. I think part of my impetus with writing the book was I didn't want to write about loneliness as this personal experience that's the fault of the individual. I wanted to think about the ways in which it can be also inflicted by societies; that if you don't fit in for reasons of race, for reasons of sexuality, for whatever it is, you're made enormously isolated by an antagonistic society.

Wojnarowicz is one of the great prophets of that. There's no shame in not knowing who he is for the very simple reason that he died of AIDS in 1992 at the age of thirty-seven. So there was a long period in which he really had fallen out of history. But he's making a huge resurgence now. He was a gay man. He'd come from a violent family. He'd been homeless for a long time, and he began to make art in the seventies and then really came to prominence in the East Village art scene of the 1980s. So alongside people like Nan Goldin, like Basquiat and Keith Haring, that sort of scene. He was mostly known as a painter in his life, but he was also a photographer. He made films, he was an AIDS activist, and he was a performance artist. And he wrote one of the best books ever written, which is called *Close to the Knives*. So he's this wonderful figure, and the reason that he looms so large in the book, apart from that I love him so much, is that he makes very clear the reasons that people can end up being very isolated. He was a person with a great deal of friends. He had a lover. He was in a community. And yet he experienced deep feelings of loneliness knowing that his sexuality made him a target in the world. There was a point when we could think, 'Oh, well, that was the eighties. Those days are gone.' And I'm sorry to say, I'm sure other people in here are mourning as much as I am what happened in Orlando [the mass shooting at the gay club Pulse on 12 June 2016, in which forty-nine people were killed]. Those days are not gone. Those days of violent homophobia are not gone.

**AB:** There's a lot in the book about not having the language to form these kind of intimate connections with people. It seems to me there has been a change in that respect. There does seem to increasingly be more of a vocabulary for people who don't fit into the normative definitions prescribed by society. And yet, as you say, there's that awful contradiction. We've made these advances and yet something like Orlando can still happen.

I saw this young British journalist, Owen Jones, on television the other day, who was having real difficulty getting commentators to accept the homophobia behind these killings. I was watching that in the context of having read your book quite recently and just thought, 'yeah, maybe there have been changes but the vocabulary is still not mainstream'. It's still hard to be heard.

**OL:** Yeah. I saw that scene of Owen on Sky News yesterday as soon as I woke up and I found it absolutely devastating, because it brought up so much of that feeling of your experience being made invisible by a society that refuses to take it seriously. He's saying 'my people were killed. This is the worst killing of gay people since the Holocaust'. And the hosts are saying 'it's not gay people, it's just people'. And he's saying 'it's gay people. They killed gay people'. It's the same thing as when people say 'Black lives matter' and other people say 'all lives matter'. Of course all lives matter! But there are some lives that are more vulnerable than others. And those are the lives we're talking about. So yeah, I think that was a reminder of how the forces of invisibility and silencing are very much at work. If you don't see that you're lucky. It doesn't mean that they're not at work, it means that you're not seeing it.

**AB:** Coming back to the work of Wojnarowicz, masks feature quite prominently. Similarly, Warhol was someone who kind of created this mask with his wig, with the glasses that he wore. It reminded me that the root of the word persona comes from the Latin for mask. So you find this sort of disconnect, in that people who are isolated from the societies they live in are forced to adopt these masks in order to try and engage with the people around them.

**OL:** Although I think in some ways what David is doing with that mask is putting that outside of himself. I think he was somebody who was very good at being incredibly honest about his experience. I don't say this in the book, but he'd lived in Paris for a long time. He was very embedded in French culture. In that series of photos of men, all with the mask of Arthur Rimbaud from the cover of *Illuminations*, that famous boy's face posed in the meat markets of New York, in Times Square at Port Authority bus station – he's this dream figure, really. He's sort of unreadable, unreachable, and also very powerful. It's playing with the idea of being not visible and what that would mean.

**AB:** Almost like the superhero's mask in a way. There's a sort of a defiance and a strength behind it.

**OL:** But at the same time, no one can reach him and he's alone. So yeah, it has both sides of that mask-ness.

**AB:** This sense of the mask and of being alone brings us on to technology. Warhol really embraced technology. For him he said it made him feel less alone, recording his diaries on tape and things like that. It gave him a way to engage with the world. But you talk quite a lot about modern communication technology, about Twitter, Craigslist. Do you think the nature of loneliness has changed with the development of the internet?

**OL:** Absolutely. And I'm not a black and white person about the internet at all. I spend a lot of time on it. I'm very active on Twitter and I think it's an extraordinary space for making connections, for making friendships, especially if you're physically isolated. If you're not around people you can make relationships across this medium, and that's wonderful. At the same time, I think it's a deeply socially competitive space that asks people to perform a kind of socially rich life that is often out of people's reach. The pressure of that, especially I think for young people, is crippling. It's so hard to keep performing this level of 'I'm so happy, look at my Instagram, look at my friends, we are beautiful'. That need to compete like that can make people feel very isolated. And if they don't feel that they possess that kind of life or can make it manifest with the right filter, then it's very lonely.

**AB:** When I think back to when the internet was starting, it was celebrated as a place where people who had social difficulties could go and, from behind this mask of anonymity, experiment, play with identity. Truly connect.

**OL:** Those things are definitely true. But at the same time, there's a longing for a kind of intimacy that has to happen in a physical space. That has to happen when you take your masks off, when you let yourself be seen in less bright, flattering light. So it's complicated in the same way that the world is complicated or cities are complicated. I just think it's insane to try and say the internet is good or bad as a social space, because it has so many threads to it.

**AB:** And, in fact, you draw that connection between the internet and spaces. There's a moment where you refer to Craigslist as the Times Square of the internet.

**OL:** Lovely sleazy spaces.

**AB:** Yeah, I guess you mean Times Square as it *was* rather than as it *is*.

**OL:** Yeah, absolutely. I'd been writing a lot in the book about the old Times Square of New York, which was the place where sex workers went. It was the sex and crime hotspot of New York. And it was a place where a lot of people had encounters. Sexual encounters, but also intimate encounters. It's a casualty of gentrification. It's been cleaned up, it's been Disneyfied – literally, because it's all owned by Disney now. So what you're going to encounter there now is like giant Sesame Street figures, and cops. I think what I was saying about Craigslist was that unlike some dating sites, which feel very gentrified, Craigslist was very, very raw. People were just saying what they wanted, which was basically precisely the sex they wanted. It wasn't dressed up as the sort of nice date they wanted to go on first. I guess I got a kick out of the honesty of it. It felt appealingly authentic and raw in a way that Manhattan often isn't because it's so much about image. So, yeah, I liked it.

**AB:** I could go on for hours, but one last thing I'd like to ask you is about the reparative function of art. One of the things that I think comes across so much in the book is how being in the worlds of these artists, learning about them and being around their work, almost acted as a cure for the loneliness that you were experiencing in New York. This is interesting because one could think that the cure for loneliness might be finding that intimate connection with another living person.

**OL:** I think I'm wary of the word cure because I didn't want to write a book that was like, 'Oh, here's my experience of loneliness. And at the end, guess what? I met someone and it's all fine now.' What I wanted to do was try and understand what loneliness was like and if there was anything redeeming or beautiful about it in its own right. So I think the cure wasn't for loneliness. The cure was for shame. And the shame of loneliness is the component that causes the pain of it. Loneliness in itself is a tender feeling, of longing for love. It's got a kind of beauty and vulnerability about it. The shame of loneliness is agonising, and I don't think there's very much that's redeeming about it at all. So what these adventures in art did for me, looking at these people's lives and understanding the many, many social forces that made people lonely, was make me realise that there's no shame about it at all. David Wojnarowicz died of AIDS. Before that he was an AIDS activist, and the social stigma around AIDS was agonisingly lonely and isolating for the people affected. And it's hardly just confined to people who have AIDS. It's the homeless, it's refugees. It's all kinds of people who experience that stigma. Those are the sort of forces that make people lonely. And I think the art that I was looking at awakened me to that. That was what was so healing. It wasn't that I needed to get out of the experience. It was that the shame needed to stop.

# Marlon James

## *A Brief History of Seven Killings*

Wednesday 6th July 2016

~

**Adam Biles:** There are some books that one reads and there are other books one inhabits. *A Brief History of Seven Killings* is the second kind of book. This is in part because of its length – it's a sprawling, lyrical epic that takes the reader on a journey from a fateful couple of days in Kingston in 1976 to New York, England, Colombia and beyond decades later – but also due to its extensive cast of characters. Every voice is pitch perfect and draws the reader into Kingston life, into the feuds between political factions, the misery of the ghetto, the attempt to assassinate an icon, and the fallout years later from this attempt. Blending real life events and personalities, with *A Brief History of Seven Killings* Marlon James has written a whole world into a novel. It's a scintillating read from beginning to end, and won Marlon James last year's Booker Prize from a shortlist overcrowded with talent. Please welcome him to Shakespeare and Company.

**Marlon James:** Thanks for coming out. It's kind of epic being in Shakespeare and Company. It's like a major bucket list thing accomplished. There are quite a few characters in my book, a lot more than seven. You should also know, if you haven't read it, that there are a lot more than seven killings and it's not brief.

**AB:** I'd like to begin at the beginning. Because one of the things I kept thinking when reading *A Brief History of Seven Killings* was how does a book of this scale, a book with so many stories, so many voices, start? Was there a first voice that came to you or a first idea?

**MJ:** If you turn to page 458, you hear the first voice that came to me. It started out being this crime novel set in Chicago and Miami with this hitman from Chicago who was given this assignment to kill this Jamaican drug lord, except he's going through boyfriend trouble. He's in love. That's how it started. But I just ran into a dead end writing that book. I thought, 'the solution is to just find another character'. So the second character I think I came up with was Bambam, the fourteen-year-old gunman. And the same thing kept happening. I kept thinking, 'I'm here to write a small book. I can't find a character to write a small book with.' Then a very good friend, Rachel – who's actually no longer with us – we had dinner, and I said to her, 'I don't know whose story this is.' And she says, 'Why do you think it's one person's story?' So I went back and read it, and it was the big eureka moment that it wasn't one person's story. The good thing about that is that since I had like 400 pages already written, I already had half a novel. But that's when I realised it was this multi-person narrative. And even then I still didn't know what shape it was going to take. At first I thought it was going to be an oral biography, like that biography of Edie Sedgwick or something like *The Savage Detectives* – it's different people, but they're talking about pretty much the same event – and it didn't turn out that way at all. For a good two thirds of that book, I had no idea that's where it was going. I had no idea this book would end up in the eighties, much less the nineties. I had no idea that some characters would make it to the end of the book, because I really intended to kill off everybody. I became really interested in the afterlives of these characters. Where do they go after this? What do you do when you run away from home and you can't return? That's how it happened. It really was . . . I like to say 'organic', but I really mean 'crazy'.

**AB:** At a moment, the character Nina says that the problem with a book is that you never know what it's planning to do to you until you're too far into it. When I was reading, I did wonder if that was a little bit your experience too.

**MJ:** With my previous book, I hated that because I had this idea that I'm the Grand Poobah of this novel and how dare characters have inner lives. It's my book. With this book I kind of let that go. My whole rule was that at the end of the writing day, whenever that ended, there must be a point where I go, 'I didn't see that coming'. And that's how it became. Also because most days I only wrote one character. Each day was sort of a surprise. I'm a big plotter, funnily enough. I write plot charts and all of that and then I promptly ignore it. I just like to get that stuff out of my head.

**AB:** So there was a moment after you set off and you weren't sure where it was going. Was there then a moment where it gelled and you realised, OK, I've got something here?

**MJ:** Well, yes and no. It kind of gelled, but also the whole time I was going, 'What the fuck!' This is how I came to peace with what I was doing. I just said, 'You know what? I'll leave it in until my editor takes it out.' And he didn't take out anything, which scared the crap out of me. So then I took stuff out. In fact, this book is 10,000 words shorter than the edition my editor was going to send to press. We still argue about that. The first thing I did was go back and make sure I killed all the adverbs because I hate adverbs. I think one or two are still in there, which really pisses me off.

**AB:** An editor that actually wants 10,000 extra words is a rare breed.

**MJ:** Oh yeah, he was all about it. But it wasn't a chapter or a paragraph. I really did sort of chop on a line by line, word by word basis.

**AB:** Let's talk a little bit about the setting, particularly of 1976. For me, it wasn't a period I knew that much about. So the book for me was as much an education as an entertainment. But you were born in 1970, so you were six years old when the event that's central to this book happened.

**MJ:** Yeah, but when I was six the conflict for me was who's your favourite Charlie's Angel, you know, things like that. Pretty much any six-year-old's world is this world of wonder. What do I remember about the attempt on Marley's life? I remember the news report because it came on at ten and we were supposed to be asleep. I remember my parents were watching a TV show and they interrupted it. You can see my sense of values, how I say that a TV show was interrupted as opposed to the most famous Jamaican got shot. So I remember that. And it was this very, very stern voice: 'Bob Marley has been shot.' I also remember it was one of the few times that I think both of my parents were genuinely uneasy. At six years old, you still think your father is Superman or your mother is Wonder Woman, and you expect them to be perfect and invincible. You don't expect to see things like fear. I never forgot that. I register it as that moment when even my parents lost their cool. And my parents are both pretty chilled people. It wasn't just an attack on Marley, it was an attack on his house. And 56 Hope Road was a sort of sanctuary in Kingston. Men who would have been trying to kill each other the day before would be playing dominoes there. It's just about the only place in Jamaica where you would find somebody who has murdered seven people, the Prime Minister of Jamaica and Keith Richards all on the same veranda. Or Roberta Flack or whoever. Some member of ABBA. It was this sort of sanctuary, this half holy, half hedonistic place. So it was as much a violation of the house as it was a violation of him. And I think for a lot of Jamaicans, the idea that if they could shoot him, they could shoot anybody – because there was an unwritten rule that nobody touches the top gun and somebody touched him. I think a lot of people lost a sense of safety after that.

**AB:** It wouldn't have resonated to six-year-old you, but in the political context as well, where you had an election impending, and the day after the shooting took place there was supposed to be this great peace concert. Do you think the fear you felt from your parents was even wider than an attack on this icon?

**MJ:** Well, yeah. I couldn't understand it, which to me is a sign that it was wider. It's of a scope that I just can't grasp when my entire world is the 400 yards to school. It's not just a sense of danger, it's a sense of wide danger. It's a sense of hearing things that I don't understand. People talking about things like Home Guard, which was Jamaica's – blissfully, mercifully short – flirtation with its own Tonton Macoutes. I mean, I'm six. I can't process any of this, but I still can tell that something changed. Part of it was also the election. It was, even by our standards, a very bloody election. The one that came after that was even worse. Most of this I can tell you in hindsight. There's a scene in the book where one of the characters, Josey Wales, is given this propaganda colouring book called *Democracies For Us* . . . playing on 'US'. I remember getting that colouring book, and I thought it was the weirdest thing because on the democracy side you get to colour rainbows and ice cream and on the totalitarian dictatorship side you get to colour long lines of ugly people waiting for bread and broken roads and all of that. This is what they were giving us at six. I'm six years old and I'm fighting the Cold War, which is ridiculous.

**AB:** That's the even wider context, of course. The US interest in the Caribbean, Cuba in particular. One of the things about the way you handle politics in the book is that it's very present, but there's no sense that you're being didactic. There are no moments where we feel we're being instructed on the intricacies of Jamaican politics.

**MJ:** It's weird. I actually think it's a very bad reason why I came off so effortless, because we grew up taking partisanship for granted. It's interesting watching partisanship turn America into this comedy of errors and Britain with their stupid Brexit, because a lot of immigrants will say, 'you know, we left our countries to escape this shit'. I took it for granted that if I'm going to a certain neighbourhood, I should not be wearing green because orange is the colour there. And vice versa. Things that nobody should ever take for granted in a country because partisanship is not something you should ever take for granted. That became just a way of life. So I think the reason why the politics comes across so easily in the book is because it had so seeped into everything that if I'm talking about somebody going down a street, it becomes a political statement in the book. When Nina says, 'I hate politics and I hate that I have to know', it's pretty much me saying that because it just filtered into everything in my grandmother's house. There were no pictures of me. But there was a picture of the prime minister, which is some stupid shit when you think about it.

**AB:** One of the things that struck me about the figure of Marley – and you touched on this a little earlier – was just how important he was. Obviously, he's gone down in history as a very important figure of the music world, but he was also very important in politics. He was seen as a unifier of the two sides, as someone who could bring peace to Jamaica.

**MJ:** It's funny that they tried to kill him in 1976, because he really got powerful in 1978, as that's when he really got political. But yeah, the Marley assassination attempt is almost like Kennedy. Nobody really knows for sure, but he was becoming important politically for all the wrong reasons in Jamaica. I think the idea that the voting populace should think for themselves was a really radical concept. My grandmother, as I said, had a picture of the prime minister on our wall. A political decision is not what you think about, it's something you're almost born into, and the whole idea of thinking independently . . . he was such a challenge to the status quo in so many ways. His hair was a political statement in Jamaica. To the extent that a lot of really rich kids would grow their hair like man, just to spite parents. His hair was, you know, using reggae as a political statement, speaking in patois on television, because Bob Marley don't sound like me when he's on TV. He wasn't trying to be political, but it became a political statement, and it still is.

**AB:** I was wondering about your decision to write him into fiction. For a lot of the book, he's quite a distant figure, the characters are circling around him, or being influenced by him, or reacting to things that he does. His actual presence in the book is quite ghost-like.

**MJ:** He is quite ghostlike even before he dies. I actually wanted my experience of Marley in the book, and my experience is like most people in the world's experience of Marley: it's records, videos, news reports, articles. It's never him unless you saw him live. I didn't see him live. So I wanted that presence. But I also was more inter-ested in all the characters hovering around him. Gay Talese has this amazing piece 'Frank Sinatra Has a Cold'. He went to LA, I think, to interview Sinatra, and Sinatra wouldn't talk to him. He kept getting this excuse 'Mr Sinatra has a cold'. What he did, and almost accidentally revolutionised journalism, is that he just interviewed everybody around him. And he came up with this amazing portrait of Sinatra without ever talking to him. That was a big influence as well. I was more interested in all the people hovering around him and what they want. And it turned into that kind of book.

**AB:** You said Marley still has a big influence today. He still resonates. Was there any apprehension on your part of approaching him as a subject for a novel, about how it would be received in Jamaica and elsewhere?

**MJ:** There's apprehension every day. People keep saying I'm brave. I'm not brave, I'm dumb. I was worried about that all the time. One of the things I made sure of is that I don't put anything in his mouth that he didn't actually say. To make sure that it's a person saying he said it, or the person just outright lying. In that sense, I was very careful about it. But I also knew he won. He comes off pretty well in the book and it ultimately wasn't a story about him. The book goes on till 1992, and he dies in 1981. So I knew he was more this kind of springboard to talk more about Jamaica but also 1980s New York.

**AB:** And the reference to him as 'The Singer' throughout. Was that again a way to keep some distance? Or was that how people referred to him?

**MJ:** No, nobody refers to him as that. I just wanted something that reinforces how iconic and symbolic he was. I mean, Prophet would have been too pretentious. But to most of us he's a symbol. We don't know him. We have no idea what he smells like, how tall he was or whatever. And that's what I wanted.

**AB:** One of the things that readers will notice immediately when they open the book is the use of different Jamaican dialect, different patois, which are very subtly different between different people of different social classes and different positions and different educations. The first thing that really impressed me was the trust you place in the reader to go with that. Because there's no apology for it. There's no making it easy. But once you do get into the rhythm of it, once it flows for you, it really increases the intensity of the reading experience.

**MJ:** I don't know if I was being trustful as much as just being crazy. This was a book where I wanted more than anything else that the book that's in my head comes on the page. I think for a lot of writers a lot of interference happens between those two stages. Some for the good, a lot of it not good. You start to second-guess yourself. You start to get too tentative. You have these minor failures of nerve. You don't go as far as you want to go or as extreme as you want to go. I was like, 'You know what? The book that's in my head is a book I want.' After a while, I just started to stop caring whether people would get it or not. I like that Junot Diaz doesn't translate his Spanish in his books, because I don't think there's anything wrong with giving a reader some work to do. The risk I was thinking was, I hope they catch on by at least page fifty, and I think most people do before that.

**AB:** It's not just the different dialects, but also just the sheer number of voices. And it's all first-person. You said you wrote a different character every day? Just keeping on top of these different characters and assuming each of these voices must have been exhausting.

**MJ:** That's why I had charts on the wall. I had to have charts to keep track of. Nobody else was going to try to remember everybody. That's too much hard work. I don't know if I'm a lazy writer but I really love to not write. So I had charts. Different characters down there. Down here, columns: different times of day. And what everybody is doing. I just needed to keep track. What is everybody doing? Josey Wales is killing somebody; Weeper is having gay sex, but nobody knows. So even though most of those things actually didn't appear in the book, I just sort of needed it. I was like some school hall manager or something. I just needed to know what everybody was doing so I could come in and out of their stories.

**AB:** Was there any sort of morning ritual to get in the mind of the person you'd chosen to write that day?

**MJ:** Oh, let's see. Burn some incense, pray to Satan. The usual. I'm a big believer that when I write, I show up to work. I always like that about Hemingway. I like that the reason why he walked around with a typewriter is that whenever he sits down, he shows up to work. And that's how I look at it. I really do look at writing as a job. Because honestly, when I get into it, the writing really couldn't care less what kind of day I'm having. I sit down and I go to work. Then I crash and burn afterwards and cry about my miserable life.

# George Saunders

## *Lincoln in the Bardo*

### Monday 20th March 2017

~

**Adam Biles:** *Lincoln in the Bardo* is an inventive comic and humane imagining of the night President Abraham Lincoln, grief-stricken at the death of his eleven-year-old son, spent in a Georgetown cemetery. The result is an astonishing book for which the term historical novel cannot do justice, replete as it is with profound and surprising contemporary resonances. Please welcome George Saunders to Shakespeare and Company.

**George Saunders:** Hello. Thank you so much for being here tonight. Isn't it an amazing space? This sacred place that's been dedicated to thinking and freedom and brotherhood and sisterhood for all these years. So thank you so much for coming. And thank you Shakespeare and Company for having me here. It's a lifelong dream to be here.

**AB:** Now I gave a short description of *Lincoln in the Bardo* in my introduction, but could we begin by hearing how you would describe the book, and a little bit about how it came into existence?

**GS:** We were up in Washington, DC, and there's this thing called the Rock Creek Parkway that runs by a cemetery. And my wife's cousin gestured up at this hillside, at this one crypt, and she said, that's where Willie Lincoln was buried in 1862 for three years. And then she added this little strange detail that I almost couldn't believe at the time, which is that Lincoln had been so heartsick about his son's death that he actually went into the crypt on several occasions to hold the body or to somehow interact with it. So that really was so moving and so deep. And I kind of thought, 'Oh, that should be a book.' But I had a writing teacher who had told us that if a young writer could tell the difference between the story she should write and the story she should think about writing, she could save herself, like, fifteen years of wasted effort. And that idea seemed to me, at the time, like one I shouldn't try to write; it was a little too emotional and too straight. So, I just kept putting it off. Finally, in 2012, I had written this book called *Tenth of December*, and it was done. And I was in that weird period, three or four months before the book comes out, when your energy is kind of anticipatory about that. And I just thought of that Lincoln idea again and had this argument with myself about why I wouldn't write it. And the reasons were like: 'Well, first of all, it's too much about love and loss and grief and everything that actually concerns you in your real life. So don't write that.' It was a little scary, actually. It felt like it would involve a truly new approach for me. So I felt myself to be at a bit of an artistic crossroads. Like either I was going to stick with the old tricks and try to make sure I didn't screw up my 'career', or I was going to risk everything. And it seemed like to *not* try would be a form of artistic suicide.

It's a very odd book. If you look at it, it looks like hundreds of monologues. In a sense it looks like a play on the page. And it takes place all in one night. Most of the narrators are ghosts. I kind of considered making Lincoln the narrator and then, you know, 'four-score and seven minutes ago, I did come in to yon graveyard' . . . I did not do that. I felt this book needed a little bit of historical grounding, so it has some verbatim historical quotes from history books.

**AB:** When I was deciding how to structure our conversation, I wrote a whole list of the things I wanted to talk with you about. When I started dividing them into groups, they kind of fell quite easily into two. One I labelled 'Lincoln', and the other one I labelled 'Bardo'. So let's begin with Lincoln. You said this story of Lincoln going to visit Willie's crypt was something that you'd heard about twenty years before writing the novel. But you also said you started it in 2012. This was, of course, at a very particular moment in American history. It was after the first mandate of President Obama, a president who evoked Lincoln quite a lot in his rhetoric, both deliberately and also maybe unconsciously. Do you think it was partly the spirit of the times that pushed you to write this novel at that moment?

**GS:** It might have been. One of the things that I loved about the eight years we had with President Obama was that, for the first time in my life, I actually thought we could maybe get there. We could maybe actually do what the Constitution told us to do. Which was to treat total equality as a birthright, not something that one group was giving to somebody else as an act of charity. So when I first thought of this book, I thought: wouldn't it be lovely to write a book about this big turn in American history? When we first started to really think we could fulfil our potential, and then it would be beautifully completed, this great national project. That was the thought anyway. So imagine my surprise . . .

**AB:** I suspect we'll get on to the cause of this surprise towards the end of our discussion. But I'd like to rest with Lincoln, for now. I'm fascinated by how you got to know Lincoln as a historical figure, but also as a character. How did you find your way into his thoughts? Into his voice?

**GS:** Nobody knows Lincoln. Nobody knew Lincoln when he was walking around. That was one of the things people said: he's an incredibly generous, kind person, but he's very private. So I think part of what you do is to learn enough about the historical facts and the outline of the person, and this allows you to make a kind of a Jell-O mould, essentially, that you know you have to sort of stay within. Then you take your own phenomenon; in my case, the love I have for my children, the self-doubts I have, the ambition I have . . . and then you kind of melt all of that down and make it into a Jell-O and you pour that into that mould. So the only real game is not to 'be faithful to' Lincoln, or make a true Lincoln – it's to make *the illusion of a Lincoln* so that the book will move the reader. For me, that incident of the father holding the son . . . everything was in that. I always kept the picture of Willie above my desk just to remind me of what the book was really about. I didn't want to dishonour him or his memory. What's the point of a novel? It's actually not to get everything right. It's not to catalogue a historical period. It's not to show the truth about the Civil War or even the geography of a graveyard. It's to kind of put the reader into that state where she goes, 'Shit, woah!' To find ourselves in that kind of irreducible, non-conceptual state of wonder that we go into after receiving a good work of art. That, actually, is the only endgame.

One thing I learned was if you want to do Lincoln, it's kind of like doing Jesus and it's very, very risky. So you want to do it for as short a time as possible. Don't keep Lincoln on stage for 400 pages. You let him come in, be there briefly, and it's like, 'Thank you, off you go!' The other thing was, there had to be not so much focus on what Lincoln would do, but on what would *any* father (and husband and middle-aged dude) do if he had just held the body of a loved one? I was not making Lincoln, but a representation of Lincoln that would be good enough not to stop the reader from believing in the action of the book.

**AB:** While the historical Lincoln wasn't necessarily driving you as a novelist, history did gift you this narrative coincidence. Which was that on the day that Willie was laid to rest, the casualty lists from the Union victory at Fort Donelson were publicly posted. Which were one of the early signs, as I understand it, of the level of deaths that the Civil War would result in. So even though you didn't feel constrained by this history, were you guided by it?

**GS:** The whole Lincoln story is so biblical, you know. Here's this guy who comes out of nowhere. His election to the presidency guarantees the South's going to secede. The war expands from a kind of a theoretical thing about union to the most important anti-genocidal battle ever fought on the continent. And then at the very moment of victory, he dies . . . on Good Friday. It's unbelievable.

The book is set within a moment when people were saying: Oh, this will be over in a couple of weeks. Then, right about this time, they're getting these weird reports by telegraph: 3,000 dead in one day, 10,000 dead over a few days. Everybody starts to realise this is a war that nobody's going to get out of cheaply. In the middle of that, the guy who's suddenly in charge is known as a screw-up. His was a corrupt government. He was having hundreds of people into the White House to have meetings with him as the war was going down-hill. Just civilians. You're that guy. Everyone's making fun of you. You're somebody who doesn't know how to do the job. Then . . . your son dies. I kept thinking of how in this situation, if you're Lincoln, you're so heavily laden with sorrow that you can't even keep up the pretence of having control of your life. You don't even have any relation to control. There's a kind of a beatific state that can happen, I think, at least from some small examples I've had in my own life, where the stuffing gets kicked out of you and suddenly all of your illusions of control fall away. I think that's the state he was in. Of course, I don't know. But then you see a turn in him after this thing, after his son's death, and suddenly (my view is) his empathy kind of broadened outward. Instead of just thinking about winning the war for his side and the northern soldiers, he started thinking about the millions of Americans who were being enslaved. He really started thinking about them. You know, maybe for the first time. His sympathy even extended to the South. But I'm not sure my interpretation is right.

**AB:** There's a moment where he's described as, I think, the saddest man in the world. I guess it's that moment when your feet touch the solid ground of absolute desperation.

**GS:** We've all had those moments. I think mostly for me, it's happened when someone I love has died. But I think it also happens when you fall in love, or you have a child, and you see that for most of your life you're going through the world with a kind of habitual way of thinking that isn't quite correct. It's not actually enough. You know – you're out on the street in Paris and you're walking along, and your mind does this Darwinian adjustment to say, 'I'm on a street, those are trees, those are people, that's a dog.' And that's true. It's a good way of doing business, of staying alive and functional. But when you're hit with a huge loss that drops down on you, you go, 'Holy shit, I'm dying. I've been dying all along. We're all dying. We're all conditional, all these crazy consciousness-bearing machines that go around . . .' I mean, the world is way beyond our ability to grasp it. So, with grief we sometimes get a little glimpse of the truth, the truth of how things really are with us, and then the walls come back up. And I think, through art, also we get a little glimpse of truth. If we read something or hear something or see a wonderful production, our eyes open just for a minute. Then they close again. But that experience is actually sacramental because it infuses every other minute of your life with this kind of awe. We saw a glimpse of the truth and can't entirely forget it, you know. That's the idea anyway.

**AB:** The bardo, of course, is a concept from Buddhist philosophy. Now I suppose one would imagine in a story about Lincoln that if we're going to talk about the afterlife, or a sort of in-between state, one might go the Judeo-Christian route. That would have been so prevalent in the United States at the time, and still is today. So obviously there's a very deliberate reason why you went the Buddhist route. And I'm interested to hear about that.

**GS:** Well, my wife and I have been kind of aspiring Buddhists for fifteen years, and one of the things that intrigued me about the Tibetan tradition is that . . . I still don't understand it very well. So I loved the idea that if I said 'bardo', I would always be befuddling myself because I don't quite know. If I said 'purgatory', well, I kind of know what that is. Purgatory is like a hard bench. You go sit there until the end of days, until God comes and gets you. So, part of choosing to think of this as a bardo state was that it helped me assume a certain mind-state while writing. I thought, 'Whatever death is, we don't know what it is. If a meteor hits us right now, we're all going to be very surprised.' But also, some of the Tibetan tradition is so interesting. They say things that make a lot of sense and yet are totally terrifying. For example: when you die, they say your mind is like a wild horse. All the time you've been on earth that wild horse was tied to a post. Well, when you die that rope gets cut. And the habits of mind that you are enacting right this minute get super-sized. So if you're a jealous person you get *really* jealous, you know; if you're a happy person, you might get *really* happy. Of course, I'm simplifying. But this was intriguing to me, this idea that if you wanted to find out about the afterlife you could look at . . . right now.

**AB:** I'm fascinated from a composition perspective. Earlier on, you talked about the things that happen in the bardo and things that don't. How much did you follow a fixed conception of what the bardo was? And from a writer's perspective, did you set yourself certain rules or did you allow it to be a complete free-for-all?

**GS:** Early on, I thought, wouldn't it be great to write a whole novel that totally enacts *The Tibetan Book of the Dead*? And then I thought: Hmm, I'd have to study it first for fifty years, and I still wouldn't be able to stay within it in a work of fiction. So, I just took it as a spur to the imagination. One thing this tradition says (as I understand it) is that if you are, say, a strong Christian and you pray and you meditate and you think in Christian symbols, then those symbols will, of course, follow you into the afterlife, and you'll see Jesus and you'll see Mary and so on. If you're a Buddhist, you'll see Buddhist iconography. You know, I guess if you're a pro wrestling fan . . . there you go. But, at some point I said, you know, I am not going to make a catalogue here, but I can use this stuff in an almost selfish, distortive, artistic way to try to make beauty. So the one thing that really spoke to me was the idea that the bardo, unlike purgatory, is a sort of transactional state, which you can actually get out of if you have the wherewithal. So in this world a lot of the dead people, their big problem is that they don't know they're dead. They're kind of in denial. And in ghost literature, there's this riff in which you say to a ghost, 'what year is it?' And the ghost will say, you know, 'Uh, 1724?' and the medium is like, 'No, it's 2017.' Or you show the ghost a newspaper and they go, 'Oh, oh, OK.' And then they go to heaven. Or wherever. So, that was kind of an interesting idea – these spirits being trapped in that graveyard because of denial and ignorance.

**AB:** On the subject of ghost literature, I've heard you speak before about your admiration for *A Christmas Carol*, and obviously that's an example of ghosts being used to tell a morality tale. I think the morals at work in *Lincoln in the Bardo* are perhaps more complex than the sort of good–bad dichotomy that Dickens was working with. But did your admiration for that book feed into this novel?

**GS:** Oh yeah. There's a scene where Jacob Marley shows up and he's got this long chain of cash boxes he's dragging along behind him. Which is kind of like the erect member in my book (except mine's a little naughtier). But I taught that book last year at Syracuse and I think it's a perfect work of art. It's like a little beautiful machine – really wonderful.

**AB:** It's also a strange challenge for a writer to set themselves, beginning a book in which essentially all but one of your principal characters are already dead. So the possibility of narrative arcs or character development or things like that just sort of disappears. Was this a conscious challenge you set yourself?

**GS:** No! And about halfway through I went, 'Oh God!' Because what happens if there's no consequences for these dead people? Then there's no story. Nothing matters. But, in a weird way, sometimes the problem of a book starts with you. You say, 'Oh my God, this is a problem. I'm no good. I should have gone to law school. I'm a total loser.' But then if you keep working, the problem passes from you into the realm of the character. Or, it becomes part of the aesthetic of the book itself. So, in this case, the potential problem was that the two main narrative threads (Lincoln and the ghosts) had no causal crossover. Specifically, it was understood that the ghosts had no way of influencing the living. But then, far along in the process, this became exactly what the ghosts were wondering and worrying about themselves. And it became very touching. They were kind of like, 'Oh, you know, we seem to not be what we were before. We feel useless. We feel like we have no impact on anything now. It's depressing.' So they kept worrying: 'Is there any way that we can be meaningful to living people?' And, in the end, that was the question the book was asking.

This stage of talking about a book is complicated because my process is very intuitive and very iterative. I do a lot of rewriting and I never think about these things in process except in terms of revising, you know? Changing this, changing that, for sound, or for sense. It's such a beautiful process because the book turns out to be smarter than I am. During the revision process it goes, 'OK, let me defer that question to page 300 and we can ask it again then.' Or it declines to answer a general question – it wants everything reduced to specific choices, at specific places in the text. So I, as the writer, attend to those, and then – surprise! – look up to find that the book has themes and so on. It's really kind of a wonderful thing, the way it all works.

**AB:** One of the things that setting your book in the bardo allowed you to do is exaggerate the characteristics from life in death. It felt like it had lot to do with how we perceive each other, how we perceive ourselves and how we communicate. It made me think of your essay which was the title essay of the collection *The Brain-Dead Megaphone*, published in 2008. In it, you have this sense that the way we communicate, particularly in the media, is this kind of shouting at each other, this kind of high-volume, low-subtlety exchange. Now you have all life in the bardo. You have people from all different levels of society, all different conditions. And the way they're physically manifested seems to also represent the way they might perceive each other.

**GS:** I have three sort of mantras that I always recite. One is Donald Barthelme, who said, 'The writer is that person who, embarking on a task, has no idea what to do.' The second one – excuse me, there are kids here; I'll have to clean this one up a little. The poet Gerald Stern said: 'If you set out to write a poem about two dogs

making love, and you write a poem about two dogs making love
. . . then you wrote a poem about two dogs making love.' Right?
You've done what you set out to do, which is . . . somehow disap-
pointing. And then Einstein said, 'No worthy problem is ever solved
in the plane of its original conception.' So what those all add up
to is that, if you have a big artistic ambition and you do exactly
that thing . . . you're a drag, you know, you've just failed your
audience. The trick is to get into it and then let the book start
talking to you in some way. That's the ultimate goal. To surrender
to the book's will. What's scary about that (and also good about it)
is you can kind of set thematics aside. You can set politics aside.
Just attend to the text. And if you're a moral, ethical thinker and
person, if you live politically, those things will all find their way in
naturally. But they find their way in by way of this beautiful side
door, which is your subconscious, or whatever you want to call it.
So this book is, for me, hard to talk about because I really just was
trying to get the stagecraft right. Can I get Lincoln in and out of
the crypt? Can I get that done in a way that feels natural and
believable? And then, as that was happening, these thematic ideas
creep in.

**AB:** If you set out to write a State of the Nation novel, you're
never going to do something which rings true?

**GS:** Right. I tell my students this. I have a very passionate idea
about this intuitive approach, but I also know people who plan out
everything. So it's not rigid. It's not *the* method; just *my* method.
But I found out a long time ago that if I have the slightest idea of
what I want the book to be, it won't . . . be anything. Or, it will
be just what I planned for it to be, and that will be dull. So I start
with the smallest little seed crystal of an idea, and then there's an
act of faith that happens, that says, 'If it's interesting to me and I
start polishing it, it's going to sprout plot.'

**AB:** At the beginning of our conversation, you alluded to the current state of political affairs in the United States. It must be a very strange moment for you to have started the book in 2012 and to have it come out in 2017. When you started it there was a president who, one might say, had a similar stature to Lincoln and, as I said earlier, actually evoked Lincoln quite a bit. And now we have quite the opposite.

**GS:** It's an electrifying moment, because those of us who got blasé about democracy have just had a little wake-up call. I was shocked like everyone was. But now I'm feeling, you know, if your dog bites you in the groin, ultimately that's on you. You didn't know your own dog. So I'm thinking: OK, as writers, as intellectuals, what's our job? The job is to open up all of our senses, like we do, and be curious, and use our art to figure out what the hell is going on, and to push back if we feel like pushing back, which I certainly do. In the States, there's a lot of young artists, young progressives, saying, 'You know, we've always believed in empathy and kindness and compassion and mutual curiosity, but now we feel like we have to fight back fiercely, without any weakness. So: should we fight, or should we be empathetic?' And I'm like, yeah, that's the best way to fight. Empathy is an essential part of fighting the good fight. So I think it's actually a pretty invigorating time for those of us who were lulled into optimism by the Obama years. I think the election was followed by a period of liberals wailing and gnashing their teeth, and now it's time to get going, like: 'Yeah, that happened.' And actually, it shouldn't be surprising. It's not surprising to a lot of people.

**AB:** Indeed. In fact, rereading *The Brain-Dead Megaphone*, it's fascinating to see that all of the seeds are there. I had this awful feeling that if people had just read this closer, perhaps . . .

**GS:** I had that feeling myself. If they'd bought more copies we wouldn't be in this terrible mess! Ha! You know, being in this beautiful place and in this beautiful city, you're reminded that there have been generations of people who've come here, into this building, this beautiful bookstore. Why? Because they knew they didn't know enough. And they knew that if they didn't know enough, they'd live smaller lives. Not only for them, but for the people around them. They live less kindly, compassionate, empathetic lives because they were living out of small projections of a very big world. I covered the Trump campaign for *The New Yorker*, and one thing I found was, if you want to eliminate the vitriol and the anger and all that and look at it clinically, people who supported Trump tend to not actually live around immigrants, people of colour, the border, or Muslims. So why do they think the things they do? Projection. We all project – that's OK. That's human nature. But one of the reasons places like this are so sacred is that people come here to blow the shit out of their own projections and get bigger ones, and maybe they blow them up so much, so often, that they have almost no projections. I think in the absence of projections you have love. That's actually what you have. Not hearts and roses, but you have clear vision and you see every other human being as a luminous soul who's not that much different from you. So if we wanted to get away from the strict right–left opposition, which is a no-win game, what we can say is: if we want to try to persuade somebody, let's talk in terms of individual human faces, individual human dreams, on actual individuals being humiliated and embarrassed. That's the one place, when I was on the campaign trail, where I found there might be a little wiggle room. The people on the right I was meeting, many of them could better understand my ideas when I couched them in specifics (and vice versa).

# Karl Ove Knausgaard

## *My Struggle*

### Monday 28th March 2017

~

**Adam Biles:** Karl Ove Knausgaard is a Norwegian author, editor and publisher. His first novel, *Out of the World*, was published in 1998 and awarded the Norwegian Critics Prize for Literature, the first time in the award's history that a debut novel won. However, it was with the publication in 2009 of the first volume of the autobiographical *My Struggle*, that Knausgaard cemented his name in the minds of the Norwegian public and began garnering a readership of millions around the world. *My Struggle*, of which we await the sixth and final volume in English, challenges our conceptions of what both novel and memoir can do. Please join me in welcoming Karl Ove Knausgaard to Shakespeare and Company.

[Knausgaard begins with a reading from the as then unpublished *Autumn*.]

**AB:** What I was thinking when you were reading was that, compared to the six volumes of *My Struggle*, this text is going to be very much rooted in the present, and perhaps with an eye to the future. Was there a sense when you started work on this project that you were intentionally turning away from recollection?

**Karl Ove Knausgaard:** Yeah, very much so. I couldn't write about my inner turmoil any more. That would be completely impossible. So I thought, what can I do? I have to look outwards? And I did, but very, very short. Just ten metres around me. I'm writing with the objects I see in that little world.

**AB:** So again, there's an obsessiveness to it, perhaps, but a sort of a redirected obsessiveness?

**KOK:** Yeah, it is. I was writing one text each morning for a year. And I spent one hour each morning just to find out which object to write about, because what can you say about the toothbrush? Not really much. But if you have to, if you push it, then you realise you can say so many things about every little object. It's loaded with meaning. There's a kind of psychology in that too. But it's a bit different and it's more like painting somehow. It's very visual in a way.

**AB:** And in that year-long process, did you feel a change in yourself? In forcing yourself to find this meaning, did you come to understand it more, to connect with the world around you more?

**KOK:** On a small scale, yes. But I wrote *Autumn* and *Winter*, and then I started on *Spring*. And I felt I can't do this any more. It's too static. So I thought, OK, I'll set it in motion. All the objects, all the things, the family, the little girl. And it was a novel. It takes place in one day. But it is in exactly the same world. It's like this novel kind of expressed things I was working with.

**AB:** And it expanded out of that exercise?

**KOK:** Yes, and all the things disappear, they become a part of the story but not the centre. It's just a human that is the centre.

**AB:** Which makes me think; if we come back to that day in 2008 when you began writing what was to become the six volumes of *My Struggle*, did you have any sense at that moment when you put the first words on the first page that it was going to become a work of such scope?

**KOK:** No, not at all. When I did that, I had been trying to write a story about my father for, I think, four or five years without succeeding. So I had to do something. I was so desperate — I could have literally cut off my arm to just get a novel done. And then I thought, 'OK no more fiction, I'll just write it as it is.' And I did. And the thing is, it was very, very scary. At the same time, there was so much energy and intensity coming up from the text, and it was exciting and it was forbidden in so many ways. I sent it to my editor and he kind of stepped back, he called it 'manic self-confession'. It was manic. And it was a confession. But then I kind of installed narration in it, and then that was the soul of the novel. But still, I thought I would write one novel and nobody would be interested. And that made me free in a way, because if nobody's interested I can do whatever I want to do. Because nobody's going to read it anyway.

**AB:** It's an interesting decision, I think, after saying you struggled for four years to write this novel about your father, rather than changing direction; it seems you had to exorcise this story out of you somehow.

**KOK:** There were so many lines that met at that point where he died. One thing was the existential thing. The other was the physical thing, that he was all of a sudden an object in the world. Then it was the family history, then it was my history, then it was our story, and then it was my identity. But to me it was so enigmatic. Because I thought I hated him, and I did hate him and I wanted him dead. And I expressed that, I wanted him dead. Then he died.

49

And I travelled down there, and I was crying for a week. Just crying and crying and crying, So I knew I had to write about this. Why was I crying? What was that?

**AB:** What's interesting is the urge to publish as well. Because, of course, as a writer I understand this urge to get it out of your system. But from the start – particularly when you were reading back what you'd written and thinking, 'Wow, I can't do this, this is dangerous, this could destroy a lot of my relationships' – did you know that you would publish nonetheless? Or could you have written it and set it aside?

**KOK:** It's not like you're writing because you're exorcising your demons. You are writing because you're trying to create something, which is a book. That's the point. You're using yourself for a purpose. That book doesn't help you in any way, but it is kind of a good thing to create something. I knew I would publish it, but I didn't think that my family would be upset, that my friends would be upset. I wrote the novel, and then I had to send it out, because I decided to send it to all the characters involved. And I thought, 'OK, they may be a *bit* angry.' Then I sent it to my father's family and all hell broke loose.

**AB:** Once it had been published?

**KOK:** Before it had been published. Then I could take the decision: I know this is hurting my family, I don't have to publish it. But I didn't take that decision. There was no way I would not publish that book. And that's a terrible thing to discover about yourself, that you're so full of ambition. You start to make excuses to explain it to yourself and to make it into something acceptable. I did that, and I'm still doing that. But it is kind of a basic moral conflict that there's no solution to.

**AB:** You make me think of a young French writer we had here called Edouard Louis, who had published his book about his family in this post-industrial village in the north of France. One of the ways he justified it was because of the importance of the story. The political importance of telling the stories of this village trumped his family's concern of being revealed to the public. But one of the things I find fascinating about your project is that it doesn't feel that there is a political objective. It doesn't feel that there's any objective apart from art, in fact.

**KOK:** But that's the only reason you could have to publish a book. I mean, at least a novel; I couldn't publish a novel for political reasons. For me, the thing that makes the novel is the exceptional novelistic things in it. You can, of course, have politics in it – you can have a lot of things in it – but that has to serve the novel. And the only way you could say something sensible about society or about politics is to be outside of politics and outside of society, which the novel is. So yeah, it's not that I'm against political literature, but that's how I think it works.

**AB:** The classification of it as a novel is interesting in itself. In the bookstore we shelve it under fiction. And yet when you've talked about it this is very clearly your life. That distinction, I think, has unsettled readers. So when you were writing – and particularly since you published two very accomplished novels beforehand – did you feel a tension between this and, let's say, novelistic techniques and conventions: the instincts of a novelist to make everything make sense, to give everything a nice conclusion or to give everything a certain rhythm? Or did you fight against that?

**KOK:** That's a good question, because I felt literature was a way for me to impress: look what I can do. And I felt that was the problem in my life as well, that I was completely reliant on what others thought of me. This book is a way of breaking free of that. I've tried to show myself as I am, without caring what other people would think. It's the same with the style. I'm not writing this to please anyone. I just tried to write. That's one aspect of it. The other aspect has to do with what it is to write a novel, about what it is to remember. The strange thing is that I found those things very similar in a way – to write, and to remember. To create something from yourself and to write about a memory. It's almost like the same process. In the book I use all the tools of a novelist. It's not a memoir because I could write a hundred pages about two or three minutes, which is a very novelistic way of writing. The other thing is that I'm not interested in my life. I'm not interested in telling stories about my life, but I'm interested in exploring who I am and identity. When I'm writing about myself, I go to the places I go when I write novels. I'm not aware of where I'm going. I don't know what I'm writing. It's just I try to get to a place where I can't think. If I do that it's like I'm disappearing into myself. Who are we outside ourselves? That's the question. And, I think, outside ourselves we are each other. Then we are music, the things we've read. It's so many similar things. And that's the place the novel works, in the things that are between us.

**AB:** That makes me think of what the journalist Evan Hughes said when reading *My Struggle,* that it is like opening someone else's diary and finding your own secrets. It struck me as a perfect description of the reading experience, but of course not of the writing experience. I mean, this is not a diary. As you say, this is a novel. There is some sort of connection for the reader, at least on a very personal level. But also, I think, it can be quite disturbing because, as a reader, you expect certain things to have meaning or to echo throughout the text. So, for example, you might spend time talking about somebody's red shoes and our instinct is to say, 'OK, these red shoes are going to be important. He's spending a lot of time talking about that.' And then we never come back to the red shoes. And it's that negotiation between what we expect from a novel and the way, let's say, real life works, which I think is one of the secrets of what makes the book so compelling. Being constantly surprised by where it takes you, and where it doesn't.

But on the subject of memory, you have spoken about it as being incredibly fluid, incredibly unreliable. And yet you give us all these details. So can we assume that a lot of the precise details are invented?

**KOK:** Yeah. Or not invented, but the moment they appear in the text it's invented. But the details are accurate. As accurate as it is possible to be, of course.

**AB:** But when it might be the brand of shoes somebody's wearing or a picture of something on a T-shirt, is that something which appears in your mind as an image when you're writing?

**KOK:** Yeah. My starting point for this book was that I shouldn't do any research. It should be everything that's in my head. And that's it. I wrote openly that you really can't trust memories. That you have a subconscious will that transforms memory so that you are a good person, or that you didn't make any mistakes, and this is working constantly in us. So one person writing about his life, what's inside his head, you can't trust it 100 per cent because there have to be many things that interfere with the truth. That's the project. You see those levels in the book that contradict each other, and that's kind of the point: to try to look for the complexity of the identity, because it changes. But we are not aware of changing because we have no point outside to see it from. We think we have always been the same way. But it isn't like that.

**AB:** You said that we have these kind of mental mechanisms that justify or excuse our actions. It's been claimed that certain people in your life and certain characters in your book get a hard ride. But I think the person who gets the hardest treatment is yourself. There's no attempt to make the reader like you particularly, or support you if you're in a dispute with somebody. Did you have to battle against those self-justifications of certain actions in your life?

**KOK:** I don't think so. Because there is an element of writing towards someone who sees you. I tried to escape that gaze from the outside, which is a restrictive gaze most of the time, and to create a place where I was free. Which means with no 'other' in that space. Still, if you are writing, there are many elements in the novel itself that reflect how we mirror ourselves towards things. I found freedom in trying to go through the places which were very unpleasant for me. It didn't hurt very much when I was writing it, just because I was free in that space. There are many embarrassing things I was writing about. I'm very interested in shame. I am a very ashamed person. I think that mechanism is a general thing between society and the self. That's the way the self is controlled or controls itself. That's where you can feel others, in your shame. So time after time I go to the places where I'm ashamed, and try to find out what it is, because that's where the relationship with others is obvious in a way.

**AB:** You said it wasn't painful to revisit these memories while you were writing. It's not that I find that difficult to believe, but I would have expected there to be certain moments, certain experiences sitting there in front of your computer or whatever, when . . .

**KOK:** It wasn't fun. But it was possible to do it. The terrible moment arrived when I stopped writing, showing it to someone. Then it was absolutely, completely terrible.

**AB:** So the relation with you and the page, it's almost like it's not externalised.

**KOK:** If you think about things when you are on your own, and you think unpleasant thoughts, you accept it. OK, that's me – and then you forget it. It's like it doesn't mean so much because there's nobody there to punish you. You could punish yourself, of course, but it's like, that's the place where you're writing, where you are by yourself.

**AB:** So even then, there's no presence of this kind of superego judging you? Because even if you're alone and you think of bad things that you've done, it's possible to feel judged and to feel shame.

**KOK:** Yeah. That's why literature has always been an escapist thing for me. That place where I can get rid of myself and be someone else or somewhere else. I did that with my two previous books before *My Struggle*. I did that in reading. I read a lot through my whole childhood. But the point with *My Struggle* was I wanted not to escape. I would not use literature to get away. I wanted to confront life. So that was a strange experience to have. But even then a kind of selfless writing was possible, even then when you were trying to write directly about yourself.

**AB:** You've used the word freedom and you've talked about the destruction of the self; when I was reading *Home and Away* there's a line – and I'm not sure if you were saying this sort of jokingly, but you say, 'I'm a Protestant deep into my bones'. I did start to think about the religious nature of your project. Because of course, when you mentioned the destruction of the self, one thinks specifically of religions like Buddhism and Hinduism. While in Protestantism, and particularly Lutheran Protestantism, there is the mortification of the body and self-flagellation leading to some sense of grace. Is that almost what's going on here, do you think?

**KOK:** I have never thought of that myself, but that's what's interesting to write in our culture and to write in a language. There's so much coming along with that culture, so much of its thinking and ideas that you just have. I don't analyse myself in that way, but I guess it's completely possible to read it that way.

**AB:** On a personal level, is there a sense of catharsis about the events that you described through the six volumes by having written about them? Is that what has allowed you, for example, in *Autumn* to situate yourself more in the present and with an eye to the future? Or do these events still trouble you in much the same way?

**KOK:** There's no catharsis in writing. I'm sorry; it is healing in the moment, but it is also a very technical thing. In the last volume of *My Struggle*, I was writing something very, very sad for me and for my family and for my children. It was that my wife was hospitalised and I was taking my children there to see her, and it was absolutely terrible. Book six dealt with the consequences of the writing. It was possible that one of the consequences was that she had a breakdown. So I thought, 'OK, I'll write about it' – which is doing it all over again. But then I also had to revisit that place that was so terrible. And I remember doing that. I was crying when I was writing. And I sent it to my editor and he said, 'Well, it's nothing on the page, you have to do it again.' And I had to go back again and do the same thing, and he said the same thing: 'There's nothing there. It's all in you. You have to make it on the page.' There's also the relationship with my brother in book five, which was terrible. But you have to detach yourself from it somehow. And at the same time, you have to be very present in the situation to relive it. And that is not cathartic in any way. It's terrible.

**AB:** I guess that shouldn't surprise me, because one of the things we find in volume five is your relationship with writing. There are moments when you give it up. You say, 'OK, I'm not made for this. I'm going to do something else.' In a funny kind of way, these are the moments when you seem . . . not necessarily happier, but there seems to be a certain contentment. Yet you're drawn back to this process of writing, which doesn't give you any, let's say, pleasure, at least in an immediate sense.

**KOK:** No, that's true. An interesting thing about not being able to write was exactly that. I thought of the text as something outside of me, which I could construct or do whatever I wanted with, but it didn't feel connected with me. Then I met one man who is the reason for me being a writer – he's still my editor – who believed in me and made me write more. I had the discovery that writing was the same as reading. It was exactly the same thing. You go into the same place. It was not about controlling anything out there. That was such a relief. Writing is to find that place, which is the selfless place, basically.

**AB:** One thing which isn't necessarily touched upon often when talking about your work is the humour. I'm thinking specifically of volume three – this is when you were a kid and, doing the sort of things that kids get up to – but I think about the incident with the bottle and the beetle, I think of the descriptions of taking a shit and things like that. You talked about crying when you were writing, but do you ever find yourself laughing in front of your computer screen?

**KOK:** I am amused, but especially with writing about being sixteen, seventeen, eighteen because there is so much tension going on and you have to be deadpan. You have to identify with the seventeen-year-old, but there is a huge distance.

**AB:** It has to be deadpan in as much as you just have to get the facts out there?

**KOK:** It has to be on his side, even though I found it completely ridiculous what he was thinking and feeling and trying to do. All those things I could have told him: 'No, you do this and it'll be OK.' I couldn't do that. I have to follow him. But I found that book a funny book. It's a comedy.

**AB:** Before we finish I want to ask you about the phenomenon of *My Struggle*. You published volume six in Norwegian in 2011, and you're still being asked to talk about this work. To what extent do you understand the phenomenon? Every writer wants to be read, and by as wide a public as possible. But did it surprise you, the level to which people have taken to your book? And are you able to explain it to yourself?

**KOK:** I was completely taken by surprise. At first it was in Norway and it was absolute madness. Then it spread, and I thought, 'there's no way I can identify myself with this. There's no way I can do that.' I'd go to something and then I'd go back home and I couldn't have this picture of myself, which is kind of negative. But that's good for me in my writing, because there's a kind of tension there all the time.

**AB:** And can you understand it? Have you tried to explain it to yourself?

**KOK:** The only thing I can think of is that I feel attached to a book when there is the presence of another person. Then I'm drawn to it. So I think the explanation must be that there is a presence in it. You feel that there is a person here. That's the only way I can explain it.

# Colson Whitehead

## *The Underground Railroad*

Tuesday 20th June 2017

~

**Adam Biles:** *The Underground Railroad* tells the story of Cora, who escaped from the bonds of slavery on a cotton plantation in Georgia with the help of the Underground Railroad, a network which in Colson Whitehead's reimagining has assumed a physical form, complete with buried stations, steam-powered locomotives and guards. As Cora advances from state to state, however, the dream of true freedom seems increasingly elusive. Colson Whitehead's *The Underground Railroad* is not just a book about historical slavery, but confronts the terrors and threats faced by Black people in America from the pre-Civil War era up to the present day. Please welcome him to Shakespeare and Company.

**Colson Whitehead:** Howdy. Thanks for coming in this heat. I'm very honoured to be here.

**AB:** I read that the idea for *The Underground Railroad* first came to you many years ago. Before we talk about the book itself, could I ask you to reflect upon why, compared to your other novels, the gestation period for this one was so long?

**CW:** I first had the idea for the book seventeen years ago. I came across a reference to the Underground Railroad. I remembered how, when I was in fourth grade and my teacher was telling me about it, I envisioned a little subway beneath the earth. Which is very impractical. Then she explained how it actually worked. But I thought that day, 'wouldn't it be a weird idea for a book if I made the metaphorical railroad into something real?' And that is more of a premise than a story. So I added the element that each state that our protagonist goes through is a different state of American possibility, like *Gulliver's Travels*. It seemed like a really good idea, and I knew if I did it back then I would have fucked it up. So I decided to wait. I figured that if I wrote more books I might become a better writer and I could pull off the idea in the way it needed to be pulled off. At the time I was a thirty-year-old douchebag in New York, and I figured that if I was older or had adventures, I might take these worldly adventures and bring them to the book. So each time I finished a novel, I would think, 'Am I ready?' And each time the answer was 'No'. And that went on for about fourteen years, when I sold a book to my editor and I was feeling some doubts about it. So I decided to tell my wife about the Underground Railroad book. She said, 'Honey, I don't want to say the book you're working on now about a Brooklyn writer going through a mid-life crisis is dumb, per se, but the Underground Railroad book sounds really good.' So I decided to talk to my agent and tell her about the idea. And she said both ideas sounded good, which was not very helpful. But then she did something she never does, which is email me on a Sunday, and she said, 'I can't stop thinking about that Underground Railroad idea.' Wednesday was Shrink Day. I told my shrink and my shrink was like, 'What are you, crazy? I mean, we both know you're crazy, but with your issues, this book is totally up your alley.' That only left my editor, who I had already sold this other book to, and he just said, 'Giddy up, motherfucker!' which is old-school publishing talk for, 'That's a very compelling idea and we should pursue it.' So I did. And this is what happened.

**AB:** When you had the idea seventeen years ago, and then when you started writing it a few years back, was it always obvious to you that the principal protagonist should be a woman?

**CW:** Over the years, when I had it in the back of my head, I'd think, 'It's a man running away. It's a man looking for a wife who'd been sold off, a parent looking for a child.' Finally I settled on Cora, someone looking for an absent mother. And there are a few reasons. There's a famous slave narrative written by Harriet Jacobs, who ran away and spent seven years in an attic before she got passage out of North Carolina. She writes in the early part of her memoir about how when a slave girl becomes a slave woman, she enters into a new, hellish phase of slavery. Because when you're a woman, you're supposed to have babies. More babies means more hands to pick more cotton, means more money for the master. It's just a different dimension of slavery than what happened to men. That seemed worth exploring. I hadn't done a mother–daughter relationship before, and that seemed worthy of doing. And then I'd had a string of very meditative male narrators. So the voice in the back of my head said, 'Mix it up, don't do the same crap over and over.'

**AB:** As soon as we meet Cora, she comes across as a fully rounded character. Despite being so young, there seems to be a real sense of quiet determination to her, even though it's not immediately clear that she is going to going to make the break from the plantation. Did the character, her voice, come more or less fully formed?

**CW:** I started with the idea of making the Underground Railroad real. There were no characters or locale. Writing in 2015, in my comfortable apartment, it's hard to project myself into the mind of a slave who could have the fortitude and imagination and faith to run away. Trying to figure out a character who could embody all those attributes I came up with Cora, and there are two moments that were key for conceiving her in my mind. The scene where she protects Chester – why do you stand up that one time after seeing the same scene, someone being beaten in front of you? What makes a person do that? And then earlier she stands up to a bully who wants to steal her small garden that she's inherited from her grandmother and mother. Resources are very scarce. You don't have any property. So the garden is very important to her. Those two moments of determination and badassery, for me, define who she is and helped determine all the other reactions in the book.

**AB:** The French semiotician Roland Barthes talks about reality effects in fiction, devices that writers use to make the reader think what they're reading is real or could be real. It strikes me that this is almost the reverse of that. This is kind of an unreality effect, because we know that the Underground Railroad didn't exist as an actual railroad network. You're clearly giving the reader a sign that what you're doing is not straightforward historical fiction.

**CW:** Immediately from its very conception there was going to be a fantastic element. All the stuff I do in the book I couldn't have done if it was a straightforward story of a slave running north. Once she gets on the railroad, we're in the fantastic element, and I can move historical episodes around to create friction and make a new reckoning with what they mean. But before she does get to the railroad, I did want to have Georgia be as realistic as possible. That means it's brutal and a lot of terrible things happen. Before I started deforming reality, I wanted to get it straight, to testify for my family members who went through it one hundred years ago, and for other slaves. I wanted to get it straight before changing things around.

**AB:** One of the elements in the book which testifies to the real history are the chapters that begin with adverts looking for escaped slaves. Now, I believe all of these are real . . .

**CW:** They're all real, except for the last one, which is Cora's. That's me, after I put her through a lot of stuff, trying to talk to her as a person, one to one, if that makes sense. The earlier ones are from the University of North Carolina. They digitised all their runaway slave ads. As a fiction writer, I like doing voices and imitating different kinds of speech, but I couldn't compete with the really compressed histories of those slave ads. You know, it'll say '$3 reward for my slave Bessie, who ran away for no reason'. Of course, we know why she ran away. 'She has a burn on her arm.' How did she get that burn? Also, there's a guy at the newspaper, whose job is to write these things. The enterprise of slavery was so vast that it captured everyone, not just the enslaved and the enslavers, but a guy at a newspaper who I assume was trying to move ahead and write articles, who had to coach slave masters on the language for a very terse and efficient runaway slave ad.

**AB:** Earlier you mentioned *Gulliver's Travels*, and I can certainly see the comparison. But one of the things with *Gulliver's Travels* is that it's such pure fantasy the reader would never think any of it actually happened. One of the unsettling things about your book is this blend of real and fantastical elements. During the first stop in South Carolina, there were a lot of moments when I felt like looking it up, to find out if it actually happened.

**CW:** I made the choice to have each state be different. I had to come up with a culture for each one, and what it said about America or freedom. I'm not actually a big *Gulliver's Travels* fan. But when I talked about this book for many years, I'd say 'different states of America' and people were like, 'Oh, that sounds stupid'. Then when

I said 'like *Gulliver's Travels*', they'd be like, 'Oh, I understand'. For many years, the different states were actually much more fantastic. South Carolina, where there are various genetic experiments underway, took place in a fantastic future, with hyper-futuristic DNA experiments. Then a few months before I started working on the book, I reread *One Hundred Years of Solitude*, and it seemed as if Gabriel Garcia Márquez's brand of magic realism might be a useful tool. In the book they had an interview with him at the back, and he talks about how when he was a kid he would listen to his grandmother's stories, and she would mix in mundane facts with fantastic facts with what he called a 'brick face'. He never knew what was real and what was fake. So many fantastic things were going to happen in my book, but I realised that if I did them with that 'brick face', and mixed the very mundane reality of slavery with the fantastic, absurd moments, and a narrator with a 'brick face', it might work more efficiently.

**AB:** I found the effect it had on me when reading really interesting. It reminded me of the way that certain narrative songs work – songs like 'The Lonesome Death of Hattie Carroll' by Bob Dylan or 'Strange Fruit'. Then I saw at the end that you referenced David Bowie, who told stories very effectively through his songs. Is that kind of storytelling, that way of giving an almost mythological or archetypal edge to a story, something that inspired you?

**CW:** I take my influences from everywhere. I think when a chorus steps into *The Underground Railroad*, that's like a *Twilight Zone* moment. All the books I love, and the TV shows and movies and music I love, they all go in different ways. At the back of the book, I talk about some of the songs I was listening to a lot, like the Misfits. I grew up in New York City where there's always a lot of noise. There's always a car honking, or an alarm going off, or someone being choked to death upstairs. There's always noise when

I'm working. I've always played music when I work, and now I have a 3,000-song playlist, that goes from hip hop to jazz to the Clash, to the Misfits. All the songs I like keep me company and I can sing along. And I have a dance party in the middle if I need a break.

**AB:** One of the most terrifying elements of the book, and I think also one of the most fascinating characters, is Ridgeway the slave hunter. Could you talk a little bit about where this character came from?

**CW:** I find Cora a formidable character. So I wanted a formidable antagonist. It took me a while to figure out what he sounded like. For six months in my manuscript I just had 'Intro Ridgeway, TC'. Now, I'm from New York and I write a lot about New York, and I was sad to be writing a book about the South because I couldn't put New York in there. Then I read Eric Foner's *Gateway to Freedom: The Hidden History of the Underground Railroad*, which deals with the sort of spy-versus-spy war between abolitionists and slave catchers. In New York, police might arrest a runaway slave and then abolitionist lawyers would get them their freedom before the slave catcher could get there. All these various legal stratagems going back and forth. So it seemed to me that I could make Ridgeway a New Yorker for two pages. For me, he's this sort of brutal, brutish warrior philosopher with various ideas about white supremacy and manifest destiny and imperial powers. The Tennessee chapter, which in the book has been ravaged by the Yellow Plague and forest fires, is, for me, a blasted landscape for Ridgeway and Cora, a blank stage for them to interact and have a combat between their different world views. And then there's Homer. He's a Black boy of ten years who's a freed slave, but still hangs out with Ridgeway and shackles himself to their wagon every night. With that relationship, I was trying to illuminate one of the weird corners of the master–slave dynamic. There were slaves who were freed at the end of the Civil War, who stayed with their masters because they knew nothing else. They couldn't conceive of anything outside the acreage that they'd known their whole lives. That's odd to us, obviously. And then there were slave masters who were raised by an older female slave named Bessie. They might say, 'Oh, I love Bessie. Bessie raised me. She's a part of the family.' And of course they would beat Bessie, and abuse Bessie's children, yet still believe that Bessie was a part of the family. So Ridgeway and Homer become a way to discuss or illuminate a different corner of the master–slave relationship.

**AB:** I find the term 'warrior philosopher' interesting because one of the most fascinating things about Ridgeway is that he seems to embody a certain conception of the American Dream. Not that he ever uses the term, but he talks about the 'American spirit' and the 'American imperative'. He says, 'I prefer the American spirit, the one that called us from the Old World to the New, to conquer and build and civilize. And destroy that what needs to be destroyed. To lift up the lesser races. If not lift up, subjugate. And if not subjugate, exterminate. One destiny by divine prescription – the American imperative.' He embodies a lot of the dark side of what we might think of as the American dream.

**CW:** I mean, that's what makes America great: the ability to destroy, and steal, and ravage the landscape in pursuit of liberty and happiness. So yeah, that's rich.

**AB:** These are ideas which still resonate today. It's become a cliché to say that dystopias say more about our current society than they do about any future society. Do you think so-called 'historical novels' – and I put that term in very heavy scare quotes – could also be said to say more about today than the past?

**CW:** Well, I'm writing now and I can't escape that. I gave a talk last week and someone said, 'this is a historical novel, but there's a lesbian and there's a hint of S&M in a section I read'. And I was like, 'Well, maybe they didn't talk about it fifty years ago, but lesbians did exist.' Just because you're writing a period piece doesn't mean that you leave out things that weren't part of the conversation. I think different storytelling modes, whether horror, realism, allegory or historical novel, are just different ways of getting at the world. There are different tools that we use as writers to attack the world in different ways. So I've switched genres a lot, and they have their strengths and their weaknesses in terms of talking about the world. I try to find how this or that genre can provide a different register to address things.

**AB:** I ask because you said you had the idea seventeen years ago and you told us why you couldn't have written it back then. And the reasons were all very personal, about your experience and your state as a writer. But the book also seems to fit well into certain contemporary conversations. By which I mean you started writing it during the final few years of the Obama administration when the Black Lives Matter movement was really starting to get public acknowledgement. Do you think the book could have been written and published in the same way seventeen years ago, or is the dialogue more open now to discussing the kind of subjects that the book raises?

**CW:** I don't think we're really open now to discussing what's in the book. I don't think there's anything that happened in the last seventeen years, in terms of cultural events, that has particularly informed the book. I was asked a lot about Black Lives Matter when the book came out. But for me, being a Black man in America, we have these periodic discussions about police brutality when there's a particularly atrocious example of it. We talk about it for a year and then we stop talking about it. Three years later there's another atrocious example, and we talk about it, and then we stop talking about it. The fact that we have an incredible police brutality problem in America is not news. It's a feature of my reality. So when Ferguson happened, it was the hundredth of a series of those kind of occasions. In terms of me being able to write it, five or ten years ago it probably would have been much longer. When I got to the part with the Living Museum and it came out, it was only two pages and I was like, 'I'm done.' I think ten years ago or five years ago, I would have had a chapter on the curator and his curating philosophy. I would have described the building of the railroad, and how they actually pulled off this engineering model. But for me, the railroad is not what the book is about. It's about Cora getting to these different arenas where she can be tested and grow as a person, and develop her ideas of self and freedom. I've written a few books and gotten better at doing different things and lost interest in other aspects of story-telling.

**AB:** One of the most striking things is not so much the level of violence that's inflicted upon the characters, but how you express it in a very sober, matter-of-fact way. For me, that had more of an impact than it would if you had gone into very elaborate or very brutal or bloody descriptions of the violence. Was that a very conscious stylistic decision of yours, to just state the facts very clearly?

**CW:** Yeah. I talked about the 'brick face' earlier, with the realistic and the fantastic. When you read slave narratives, you see they would describe the most atrocious events in their life with a straight face, unadorned. Because if it's your everyday existence you don't drama-tise it. If you've been beaten twenty times, how can you make the twentieth any more dramatic? So there's the 'brick face' in terms of reality and fantasy, and also the 'brick face' towards the matter-of-factness of the violence. I borrowed that from slave narratives. It didn't need to be adorned because I think it speaks for itself.

**AB:** As you can hear Notre Dame is just ringing us out, so we're almost going to have to knock it on the head soon. But before we do, I have a final question. After you write a book like this, which has had such an impact – not just in terms of prizes and plaudits and great reviews, but also, as you can see from readers here tonight, on people's lives and on the culture – how does that affect you as a writer? Are you able to protect your writing instinct, your writing urge, from the sense of responsibility upon having written a book that has had such a big impact?

**CW:** Well, there's two things there. This book was hard to write, and my first book was hard to write. Really hard to write. That's not going to go away. You know, I was pretty happy in April. I heard about the Pulitzer and I was like, 'I'm going to be in the mood for a change.' And then the next day I tried to write a page and I was like, 'this sucks!' So I try to do the best job I can each time. Sometimes people come along for the ride and get it, and sometimes they don't. This is my eighth book, and definitely some books have left people scratching their heads. But sometimes, like with this book, sometimes people come along for the ride. And it's very lovely.

# Hari Kunzru

## *White Tears*

Thursday 6th July 2017

~

**Adam Biles:** The friendship between Seth and Carter – the former an introvert, the latter a trust-fund hipster – was born of their mutual obsession with music. They moved in together, set up a recording studio, and quickly made their mark on the music production scene. What follows is an electrifying, fiercely political, harrowing story of music, identity and how the forgotten ghosts of a culture will eventually rise up to enact revenge. Infused with all the humour, linguistic brio and formal invention readers have come to expect from Hari Kunzru, *White Tears* is a novel from a writer at the top of his game. Please join me in welcoming him to Shakespeare and Company.

**Hari Kunzru:** Thank you for consenting on a hot day to sit inside. Apparently, we're expecting what my four-year-old son called a 'kale storm'. So I don't know if actual green vegetables are going to descend from the sky, but he was quite excited about the whole thing. Even when I explained it was ice, the idea of ice falling on Daddy's head was also amusing . . . Anyway, thank you so much for coming out.

**AB:** *White Tears* is a book so infused with music. I remember reading the opening chapters and thinking, 'how is he going to pull this off?'. Because of course the novel is not anti-musical, but it's such a different medium to music. So I was wondering how the novel was going to balance these two elements. Was that a challenge for you?

**HK:** I can't remember this quote, so I'll probably misquote it, but it's something like: 'Writing about music is like dancing about architecture.' It wasn't straightforward for me at the beginning because I realised when I started to write that I was very dominated by my visual sense. When it came to conceptualising a scene I asked myself, first off, what things looked like. So I spent quite a while trying to train myself to increase my vocabulary and the ease with which I could describe sound. Seth has this very geeky way of talking about audio; he likes the technical side of it. But I wanted to do something much more evocative than just saying the names of what boxes something is going through. So I did what he does in the book, which is to buy this binaural recording equipment, which is amazing – these little tiny microphones that sit in your ears, which are very sensitive to where you position your head. If you listen back to it through headphones you can really hear how the person is positioned in the space. So if you walk through a crowd of talking people it's quite spectacular, the effect. If you walk around a city with one of these things in your ears, and you're monitoring it, you get a slightly amplified version of the sounds you're hearing through your ears at the same time as you're walking. What I found is that because that sound is pushed up a bit further in your consciousness, suddenly the hearing takes over and you understand places by what you can hear rather than what you can see. So I'd be walking along the street and I'd realise there's birds in the tree up on this side street in the East Village, you know. I'd lived round there for a while and I'd never have thought that. It's also very good for eavesdropping on people because nobody thinks that you're listening to them if you're not facing them. So that was one thing I did to get into this book. And obviously listening to a lot of blues records.

**AB:** Well that's the other element, I guess. It's a first-person narrative so of course it has to be convincing. I was utterly convinced that this guy knew what he was talking about, his obsession with blues music and the collecting culture associated with that. I know that one journalist writing about *White Tears* said something like, 'I fear for his bank balance because I'm sure he's got piles and piles of records at home.' Was blues music and collecting blues music something you were into before, or that you got into while researching and writing the book?

**HK:** I had got into listening to pre-Second World War music of all kinds about ten or twelve years ago. And when I moved to the States it became quite a thing. I habitually try and orientate myself in a place using history and using some reference to the past, and listening to old folk music – which is what blues is, and what country music of various kinds is – was a useful way of me understanding the people I was living with. And then I found out more about the collecting culture around blues records. It fascinated me because it is a tiny subculture populated by real obsessives. Everybody knows about record collectors and the one-upmanship and the nerdiness. But blues collectors are often dealing with records that may exist in only one or two or three copies. You're dealing with a peer group of people who have been at this, in many cases, since the fifties and sixties. So people know what each other have, and they know that X loves jug bands and another person likes Appalachian fiddle music. So perhaps if you can get that Appalachian fiddle record off somebody else and add it together with this other record, you might finally pry that copy of the Mississippi Delta blues record that you want from this other person. It's utterly inaccessible to people who have not been part of this milieu for a long time. But thank goodness – for people like me – there's the internet, because all this stuff is around. I can hear the most obscure music without having to own the record. I mean, I did make a great connection with a collector who allowed me to actually put the needle down on things that do not exist anywhere else in the world other than his listening room. It was very brave of him.

**AB:** There's a moment where one of the characters goes to a gathering of these collectors. And he says there was something like five of them in the room, all men. And of course, your two protagonists are men as well. Is there something peculiarly masculine, do you think, about this urge to collect, as well as the musical snobbery that sometimes goes with it?

**HK:** I mean, not exclusively masculine, because I know plenty of women who are very serious about music and who do collect and play. But I do think that it is a way of men being with other men without having to get into any mushy stuff. You can know people for a very long time and just talk about stuff. You can sit down and you can say serial numbers to each other and feel thoroughly emotionally fulfilled without anybody knowing anything about what's going on with anybody's life. I have a collecting impulse, which, thank God, I've never really quite expressed fully because it goes off in different directions. I make little half collections of things when I'm researching a book. It's like assembling things together. Maybe that is a gendered thing.

**AB:** A moment ago you said, 'thank God for the internet' because it meant you could hear all this music. Yet the division between analogue and digital, at least early on in the book, is something which plays quite a defining role for the characters. There's one moment where Carter dismisses something as just ones and zeroes and says, 'I think this bullshit about lossless, you know, there's always a loss'. There seems this attraction in our culture today to what we consider to be authentic.

**HK:** I think my whole writing life has been in some kind of conversation with the idea of the authentic. My gag I use a lot is that I'm the most inauthentic person I know. I fail to fully inhabit all the various kinds of spaces that I should fully be inhabiting. But I think that in our post–internet culture, cultural symbols in particular are very easily available. When I was growing up before the age of the internet, if you had a certain record or a certain piece of clothing, it had taken you a great deal of effort to acquire that. So the mere possession of that thing meant someone might be worth connecting with. But now the gap between me hearing about a band for the first time and listening to them is my typing speed, essentially. I think because of that there's a sense that everybody can mutate themselves all the time. We talk about the hipster, and the hipster isn't somebody who has a particular set of cultural allegiances. It's not like the old youth tribes, if you're a mod or a rocker or a skin. You're going to be faithful to this set of symbols for life, or so you think as a sixteen-year-old. It's more to do with an attitude towards being receptive to the new, and the latest, and who will be per-manently ahead of the curve. That's a very stressful and slightly paranoia-inducing position to have. There's that LCD Soundsystem song 'Losing My Edge'. There's this slightly aging cool guy who knows that he won't be able to maintain his position surfing the very tip of the very top of the wave, because sooner or later the younger gun is going to come and shoot him down. I think that's the condition in which we live. So the wish for something authentic and for physical objects rather than infinitely reproducible digital ones is a neurotic reaction to the internet.

**AB:** It's funny, it does seem like a very recent phenomenon. I remember being at university, you would walk into a class and you'd be able, more or less, to tell what music people listened to by how they were dressed. Then when I was teaching university students a couple of years ago that was no longer the case. The concept of specific tribes seems to have broken down.

**HK:** Cultural symbolism is working in a completely different way. I think we're only really beginning to understand that shift now.

**AB:** You deal with this in different ways throughout the novel. I'm not sure we could even call it nostalgia, inasmuch as it seems to be nostalgia for periods before these people were actually alive. So that might be, for example, the Instagram filter you use on your photos to make them look in some way more authentic.

**HK:** There was a fashion a few years ago for making everything look slightly washed out and yellow like in the work of Laszlo Kovacs, the cinematographer who filmed a lot of those new Hollywood movies in the late sixties and early seventies, getting a little bit of light into the lens. And there's a certain endless summer feel that everybody was basically buttering on top of their pictures at that point. I suppose I'd like to say the name of a friend of mine who died earlier this year, Marc Fisher, who used the term hauntology to talk about this, which is a term that he took from Derrida, actually. He was thinking about music especially but it works for other things like those Instagram filters. The idea that we get a certain cultural kick from the distance in time. If you listen to a recording that has crackle on the surface, it's impossible to ignore the fact that it's old. This is part of the way it has meaning for you. There is a fashion for that; a wish to experience that longing and that regress in time.

**AB:** This is something which Carter feels very intensely. We talked about him as a trust-fund hipster. He's from a very wealthy family. Do you think that relationship with the past and with this idea of inauthenticity is exacerbated for people who come from, let's say, extreme wealth because they're maybe more rootless?

**HK:** Yes. I think when you can wave a credit card and buy anything, then your life risks a certain thinness. A lot of rich young people I have met have that sense of their world. I mean, why do rich kids become junkies? They're looking for something that is not consumable in a straightforward way. But not everybody wants to be nostalgic. You know, you ask Americans what time period they would like to have lived in, and white Americans will be like, 'Oh, I'd like to live in 1920.' Even 1865. And pretty much everybody else is going, 'Well, I wouldn't have been in such a good place back then.' So this relationship to the past is not an innocent one. I'm interested in certain sorts of forgetting that happen. I came to live in the US about ten years ago and this book is one way of me orientating myself and trying to come to terms with the racial history that infects almost every aspect of American life and is often not acknowledged.

**AB:** That plays a very big role in the novel. There's a moment where Seth observes, 'we really did feel that our love of the music bought us something, some right to blackness'. It seems an incredibly complicated relationship between this subject of who owns the music, who has a right to interact with it, to show some proprietary attitude towards it.

**HK:** I'm very interested in the idea of cool. Obviously, that's a word with a history. It's a word which comes out of a subculture associated with jazz music and also with heroin and is about the way of being in the world that certain people who are quite outside the mainstream adopted and became attractive to people who were not cool but who wished to present themselves as cool. The blues is really interesting in thinking about all this because the paradigmatic figure of the blues musician – the Robert Johnson-like guy who goes to the crossroads and gets down on his knees and sells his soul to the devil to be able to play guitar – is this ultimate outsider. Often you get lazy descriptions of blues musicians as being these quasi-demonic figures who come out of the earth or come in from the outside. And this doesn't really mesh when you start looking at the biographies of a lot of these guys. In the twenties and thirties, people had a lot of different relationships to music. For every itinerant Robert Johnson-like character, there was somebody else who might have a strong professional career playing in medicine shows. I mean it all goes towards this construction of a Black authenticity, which young white people crave, and rich young white people crave a lot. This vampirism is attached to that, and they want the good things without the bad things. Because if you are actually outside society, then bad things happen to you and you are treated in ways that young, cool white kids would not want to be treated. As a culture more generally we are in the middle of this conversation. I was writing this book during 2014, 2015, as the Black Lives Matter movement grew in force, and it became apparent that this was the most important civil rights movement since that of the sixties. Plenty of people have known that there was unfinished business for a long time, but it became something that a lot of people who had ignored it for a long time were unable to ignore. Another thing I wanted to do in this book was attempt to connect historical dots going back. Because I look at things like the way that Ferguson, this small community which became a flashpoint after a police officer shot Mike Brown, was a place where law enforcement methods, and the way law enforcement was financed, has complete continuity with techniques of social control that go back certainly to the days of Jim Crow and further back into slavery days. A lot of people think it's slyly histrionic to make that connection. Clearly, chattel slavery is not what we're looking at today in the US. But I think it behoves all of us to really understand that there is that continuity. We have a president now in the US who started off by redlining Black families from his apartment buildings, who took out a full-page ad in *The New York Times* to try and get the Central Park Five to be given the death penalty, young boys who turned out to be innocent of the crime of which they were attacked. I mean, these people are at the very, very top of the political order right now in the States. I see this book as part of all that conversation as well.

**AB:** I think one of the driving forces of this book is, as you say, to retrace the line of history which, in the many ways people listen to and consume and obsess about music, is often broken. So Seth says one of the reasons he liked blues music was that it wasn't political. He could escape politics while listening to it. So he wants, as you said, to take the good and push away what he considers the bad.

**HK:** I grew up in London and I have my own history with race, which is much more to do with post-imperial Britain. But I turned up in New York in 2008 and there was an election campaign going on, and Barack Obama got in. I was in Harlem and was surrounded by people for whom this had a significance way beyond any other election I've witnessed in my life. And then there was a very interesting rush from the commentariat to say, 'We've elected a Black president, we are now in a post-racial America'. It was like: we can just draw a line under this and we can move on. I think America is a country that is culturally predisposed to look to the future rather than to the past. Americans don't love having their noses rubbed in the past. I mean, Brits like it because we've got the Queen and what have you. But there's a cultural preference for being future orientated and if you try and stop people and say, hang on, what went on back there, how did that money get made? Who built that? People are resistant to that. It was very interesting to me to see the indecent haste with which people were trying to consign that history fully to the past. And of course, what did we get? We got anything but a post-racial America. We got an eruption of all the suppressed horror that had been in abeyance for a period of time. And eventually it grew orange hair and took charge.

I mean, I have no business writing this book. That's an important part of this book. I have wandered into the middle of some other people's story and sat down and tried to make myself at home. The fact that I have no rights in the telling is important to me in doing it. I have my own reasons for wanting to do it, but we are also in a moment when there's a lot of policing going on of boundaries, about who's allowed to say what and who's allowed to represent what. I think often things which appear progressive get turned back on themselves and get turned away from the targets that they should be taking.

**AB:** I guess it's an absurd thing to wonder, but do you think a similar book would have been written by a white American, or by a Black American? And do you think it would have provoked different reactions because of the background of the writer? And in a way, being absented from this particular dynamic yourself, do you think that gave you a bit of a free pass?

**HK:** I don't want to say that I'm innocent or fully outside anything at all. I'm up to my eyes in all this stuff, same as everybody is. But my guess would be that it would not be an obvious route into the material for a Black American writer because this is a book which doesn't send to a Black character. It's almost about the absence of somebody who should be present. It's about the absence of a recording that should have been made. And the people at the centre of it are white people who are haunted by race and by the repression of certain truths about how they got to where they are. It's not really for me to say whether I have a free pass of any kind, but I would guess it would be very hard for a white American writer right now to write some of the racist dialogue that comes out of the mouths of my white characters, for somebody on the internet not to decide to mistake the character for the writer. There are things that I got to have characters voice in the book that are uncomfortable things, about how Black people are more authentic than white people, that kind of thing. Maybe me coming in at an angle gives me the liberty to occupy a space that others wouldn't.

**AB:** You used the word 'repression' a moment ago. It's funny that on an individual level, when we're talking from a point of view of psychology and psychoanalysis, we find it very easy to say that repression of things that happened in the past is a damaging thing, and they'll come back to haunt you. Whereas on a societal level – and not just in the United States, in Britain and in France as well – there seems to be a tendency to ignore that very healthy advice.

**HK:** Yeah, there's the Freudian opposition between mourning and melancholia. Melancholia is a state where you're condemned to repeat the same thing and not be able to move on. And, you know, it seemed to me that is a condition that we do find ourselves in because of an unwillingness to squarely face history. This novel is a ghost story in that it respects the rules of that genre. It seemed to me that we were dealing – I am dealing – with a situation where people are haunted and where people are unable to move on because the past is still present. Yet ghost stories are always about something from the past that has been prematurely buried, that rises up into the present and makes itself felt. It's no accident that a lot of American ghost stories take place in sites that were once an Indian burial ground, because there are things that have to be repressed in order to function.

**AB:** That was actually going to be my final question, about the genre choice. So as you say it is a ghost story. It is quite harrowing, quite hallucinogenic at times. When you decided to pursue that route, did you find it liberating to be able to work within the restraints of the genre?

**HK:** I mean, restrictions are usually good, artistically. I had to decide what I felt haunting was and how it would feel to be properly haunted in this literary way. I decided it would feel as if you were unable to move forward, that for every forward step you took, you were somehow taking two steps backwards. So the central character in the novel starts to have this historical slippage. I suppose he starts to feel simultaneously like there's no sense of linearity and moving on. It feels ever more static and actually the blues has a lot of vocabulary for that. Like being jinxed. There's a lot of words that come, ultimately, from African magic. There's a Robert Johnson song called 'Stones in My Passway', which comes from a way of bringing bad luck to your enemies. If you want to do something to someone else, you can put something in their way that they will walk over. That's a way that you can put a curse on somebody. There's a wonderful song which talks about the jinx rubbing around my legs like a cat. It becomes a literalisation of bad luck and trouble that is around in people's lives. I felt, the more I got to know the music and the more I paid close attention to the lyrics, that people had a very sophisticated vocabulary for talking about their condition socially, spiritually, psychologically. You know, it does bad things to your head to be on a chain gang.

# Leïla Slimani

## *Lullaby*

Tuesday 27th March 2018

~

**Adam Biles:** 'The baby is dead. It took only a few seconds.' In *Lullaby* – her Goncourt prize-winning novel – Leïla Slimani takes us deep into the collective psyche of a certain slice of Parisian society, exploring in forensic and elegant prose the layers of wealth, class, race and gender that can rub up against each other; at once, almost unnoticeably, and yet with unthinkably catastrophic consequences. Please welcome Leïla Slimani to Shakespeare and Company.

**Leïla Slimani:** Thank you very much.

**AB:** I'd like to begin with when you began writing the book. It's on record that the original inspiration for this book was a real-life case that took place in Manhattan. This is your second novel and the second novel taking a real-life event as a jumping-off point. The first one was slightly inspired by the events around Dominique Strauss-Kahn's arrest in the United States. So I'm interested in where you would situate this on the literary scale. Let's say on one end we have pure fiction – and I use the word 'pure' with lots of caveats – and on the other end, perhaps works like Emmanuel Carrere's *L'Adversaire* which try and stick as closely to the real events as possible.

**LS:** Actually, I was already writing the book when I discovered the true story. I was thirty. I had a little boy and had just hired a nanny. And I discovered this very weird relationship that you can have with the nanny. I myself was a child raised by a nanny in Morocco, and could remember how sad she was sometimes, how humiliated she felt sometimes by my parents and me, and the gap that existed between her and me. Because she couldn't read and she couldn't write. As I got older I grew closer to my mother, and was moving very far from the nanny, and I could feel that she was very sad about this. So at the beginning I decided to explore this relationship because this is the only relationship where you pay someone to love. You say to a person, 'I'm going to give you a salary and I want you to love my children. I want you to give them tenderness, and to love them and feed them and everything.' It's a very particular relationship, because there's a relation of power, of violence too, but there's also a lot of love and intimacy. Then I discovered the true story, and had the idea of beginning the book with the murder because I wanted to look – to not avoid the fear and violence in this relationship. I wanted to speak about this very particular fear that every parent knows when you have a child. The first time I looked at my child, I think the first feeling I had was not love. It was fear. I looked at this little baby and I was like, 'If something happens to him, what is going to happen to me? I'm going to die. I won't be able to deal with this fear and anxiety.' I have to act as if it doesn't exist. That's why I decided to begin with this true story, because it's like a fairy tale: a witch that kills the children. But this is not the point of the book. The point of the book is not the murder. The murder is just there to make us remember the fear.

**AB:** This fear is a feeling you give to Myriam in the book. She says that since the moment her child was born she's essentially been afraid all the time. Yet the role of Myriam is very interesting. As is often the case with women in our societies she has to shoulder the responsibility not only for deciding to have a nanny, but also for the actions of that nanny. So, for example, when they were discussing Myriam returning to work and them hiring a nanny, the discussion wasn't framed around how much money the family would lose but the impact it would have on her salary.

**LS:** Myriam is a little bit like me and a lot of the women here. She belongs to the first generation of women to whom everyone said, 'you can have everything'. You can have children. You can have a job. You can get married. Or if you don't want to get married, you don't have to. You can be an individual. You can even be a little bit selfish if you want. Today, you have it all, you're like, 'Oh my God, what am I going to do now because I have it all, but no one is helping me. No one is explaining to me how to do it.' I wanted to show how difficult it is to have it all. And that it's a little bit of a myth. It's not that easy to be an independent or a free woman. Myriam wants to do everything perfectly. She wants to be a perfect mother. A perfect lawyer. She wants to have a perfect life with her husband. That's very difficult for her because she's always disappointed by herself. She's a woman who is struggling, like a lot of women – struggling to accept the fact that she's not perfect.

**AB:** She's damned if she does and damned if she doesn't. After having children and not going back to work, she was considered in some way to be of a lower status for having made that decision. The moment she decides to go back to work and to employ a nanny, there's judgement for that coming from the same people.

**LS:** Exactly. That's something I wanted to say about women. Society always makes you feel guilty. When you stay at home, other women look at you and say, 'Oh, you don't work. That's nice, to take care of your children', but you know they despise you. When you work a lot it's, 'Oh, you don't see your children? Oh, no. I understand you travel a lot. That's very good.' And you know they despise you again. It's very difficult. I think the only way to solve this is to do whatever you want and not look at people who judge you. But you also feel this with your husband. When my husband travels, everyone tells him, 'Oh, wow, you travel a lot. You must miss your children.' When I travel, everyone tells me, 'Oh, wow, you travel a lot. Your children must miss you.' I'm the one who's missing from the family. But for my husband, it's different.

**AB:** In fact, the role of the nanny is generally seen as a sort of replacement mother. Partly because nannies are generally women, but also because it implies that the nanny isn't standing in for both of the parents who go to work. The nanny is standing in specifically for the mother.

**LS:** When I began to write the book, I asked friends how they chose their nanny. A lot of them said, 'She looked very maternal. She looked very tender and she had big boobs. So maybe she will be very tender with the children.' It's very irrational. So you're right, it's sort of a second mother but it's not the real mother. That's why this relationship is weird, because the mother wants her children to love the nanny, but not to love her as a mother.

**AB:** There's a moment when the nanny is described as a fake mother. I think in the original French, you use the word 'ersatz', which gives the sense that the nanny is in some way filling a space, but only in a quite artificial way.

**LS:** And everyone feels uncomfortable because of this, because everyone knows it's not true. Everyone is telling her, 'You belong to the family.' Everyone knows that she doesn't belong to the family.

**AB:** This leads to an interesting tension between Louise, the nanny, and Myriam and Paul. On the one hand they want her to be this replacement mother, but at the same time, for their own consciences, they want her to be as invisible as possible. This tension is quite hard for them to resolve, and also quite difficult for Louise to bear.

**LS:** I was fascinated by this question of intimacy. It's very difficult to share intimacy with someone, even in a couple. When you live for a long time with someone, sometimes they become invisible. Every day you come home from work and you see them, but you don't see them any more. This is a little different because she shares intimacy with them. She knows everything about them: what they eat, how they sleep, what they are doing, even during the weekend, even when she's not there. But at the same time, they are not intimate. They don't belong to the same family. Myriam feels very uncomfortable because she knows that Louise looks through her clothes, or sometimes takes some of her face cream. It's a very weird feeling.

**AB:** There's a moment when she doesn't come to work in the morning, and Myriam and Paul are trying to get in touch with her and they say, 'If she doesn't answer her phone soon, we'll go round to where she lives. What's her address? Let's check the contract.' There was something about that which really underlined the fact that however intimate this relationship is, they still have to check the legal documents to find out where she lives.

**LS:** Intimate, but just on one side. Not the other. They don't want to know about her. They don't want to know what her life is. There are boundaries. She's their employee and that's it. But this is not true. They know it's not true. I also think they don't want to know about her misery. They don't want to know about her difficulties because it's too much for them. They don't want to have to accept this and be obliged to help her. So she has to stay far away from them.

**AB:** It's a strange distance to maintain. That's one of the many ways this tension mounts as the book advances. One of the sections I thought was particularly interesting was from the perspective of Olivier, one of the people that Louise had cared for previously. He seems to have, again, a very ambiguous relationship, at least in his memory, with Louise. It's parental, but also almost romantic, quasi-sexual even. It made me think that we don't really talk about the effect it has on children, being raised by somebody who is maintained in this position in the family.

**LS:** It was very difficult and very interesting to build the characters of the children because I hate books and movies that show children as either innocents or as evil. Nothing is ever complex. I think children have a very complex psychology. They understand a lot of things and can use this to manipulate the adults. So I really wanted the children in the book to be like this. Children have a lot of intuition too. Mila, the daughter, feels that something is going wrong with Louise, but she doesn't have the words to express it to the adults. And even if they have the words very often adults don't believe them. They say, 'Oh, she's just a child. She doesn't understand.' And Victor says, 'I know that something could have happened to me. She could have killed me. It could have been me.' I think that children feel things like this.

**AB:** The adults feel it as well, but they have a strange interest in pushing away these feelings. This is particularly evident with Paul. In fact, at first he has this deep discomfort with the idea of having a nanny at all, inasmuch as what it says about the kind of person he has become. That he has entered into the bourgeoisie. He never really saw himself that way.

**LS:** He's the typical Bobo. He's still a little bit of a teenager. He doesn't want to become a real man. He doesn't want to become his father. He doesn't want to be a boss. He says, 'I don't want to say to someone, "I'm going to fire you".' He doesn't feel good about this, but when he hires Louise and she begins to cook and do everything in the apartment, he feels that maybe being bourgeois is not so bad after all. It's difficult for him to accept the fact that, in the end, maybe he's just like all the others.

**AB:** It's difficult for his mother to accept this as well. As I was reading I was trying to figure out Paul, where he came from, what his motivations were. Then you introduce his mother, and everything seemed to fall into place. She's a former *soixante-huitarde*, and remains an adherent to philosophical ideas of liberation, particularly for women, yet is also very judgemental of her daughter-in-law and the decision to have a nanny.

**LS:** She's very disappointed by her son and Myriam because she thinks that they are individualist and selfish. She thinks they are fakes because they say they are ecologists and that they vote for the left and everything, but she says it's not true. The way they act shows that it's not true. Even the education they give to their children is a bourgeois education because they want them to have piano lessons and do everything like the little bourgeois kids in their schools.

**AB:** Indeed, the concept of class is very present. It's interesting coming from an English perspective, where class is much more codified in society. It doesn't quite work in the same way here. All French people are children of the Revolution. There's essentially no class system in France. Yet the class system imposes itself through the way people live and the areas they live in, and how much money they have specifically. One thing that was interesting to me was reading the book in its Parisian context, and seeing all the little things that Parisians would pick up on immediately. The location of their flat, things like that. I was wondering if, despite the harrowing nature of the subject matter, you quite enjoyed playing with these codes of French society.

**LS:** Paul is me. And Myriam is me. I know the Bobos very well because I'm a Bobo. I live in a decent neighbourhood and I eat quinoa. My son goes to singing classes and blah, blah, blah. I can make fun of them because I'm making fun of myself. But as you said, I think there is no class. Myriam and Paul don't define themselves as belonging to a class. They just have values. They say: 'We believe in equality. We believe in ecology. We respect people.' So they don't belong to a class, but they have cultural values. Louise doesn't belong to a class either because she can't take advantage of any solidarity. If you belong to a class, you can have solidarity inside that class. But she's alone. She's a white nanny, so she's doing an immigrant's job. She can't be in the African group or the Philippine group. There is no *lute de classe*, no fight. Because they never fight. She says nothing. They just look at each other and act as if everything is OK. Even when they receive a letter from the equivalent of the IRS, they say nothing.

**AB:** I find the different perceptions people have of Louise depending on where they're coming from very interesting. Louise's friend, another nanny she meets in the park, says Louise could pass for a real bourgeois lady. At the same time, Paul in particular seems to despise her for her poverty, when he discovers that she can't swim and associates that with a lack of education . . .

**LS:** He thinks she's ridiculous. She tries to be a bourgeoise, with her ridiculous dress and the way she puts on makeup. Paul and Myriam don't need to put on these kinds of clothes. He's cool. She's not cool. So he despises her a lot.

**AB:** Louise is so precisely defined and so evocatively drawn that I'm really interested in the origin of this particular character. For example, you said that she's a white nanny doing the job of immigrants. So for you as a writer, it was clearly a conscious decision not to have the nanny come from an immigrant background. Would you be able to talk a little bit about the way Louise evolved?

**LS:** When I was a little girl I was very afraid of Mary Poppins. She's too perfect. There's something not good about this woman. So I was like, I have to begin with Mary Poppins. She has to be perfect. The perfect dress, acting perfectly with the children, playing with them. For me, this perfection was a way of putting a lot of anxiety into the book. So she's perfect. She has always wanted to be desired by people, to be needed by others. That's her whole life. To be needed. So she completely forgot her own life. She forgot her child. She forgot her husband. She forgot everything. She just wanted to belong to another family, another class. And she wants people to look at her and say thank you. Thank you so much for what you did. And of course, she becomes crazy. For me, Louise is like a plate. Every day you put the plate on the table and you don't see that inside the plate something is breaking. Then one day you put the plate down and it breaks. For me, she's like that. She has a lot of things breaking inside. No one sees it. And one day she breaks.

**AB:** There are a couple of things that came to mind as I was getting to know Louise. The first was this idea of the micro-humiliations in her life. A succession of very, very small humiliations. It made me think of a Bukowski poem called 'The Shoelace', in which he says it's the continuing series of small tragedies that send a man to the madhouse. Not the death of his love, but the shoelace that snaps when there's no time left.

**LS:** Exactly that, it's the little things that people do. The fact that people speak about her as if she's not there. The fact that sometimes the children say, 'I don't want to see you, I want Mum.' If every day you have children saying this to you, it's very hard. So yes, it's a lot of micro-humiliations that make her so desperate.

**AB:** Concerning specifically the choice that she would be a white nanny. Was the question for you that if you portrayed her as a nanny from immigrant origins, it might be seen as if you were in some way associating her ultimate act with, potentially, her condition as an immigrant in France?

**LS:** No, I think the first reason was that I wanted to be a little bit ironic. I think very often in the media, in the movies, and even in some novels, when you speak about someone who is rich, he's white. When you have someone who is poor, he's Black or from North Africa. The reality is much more complex. Now in our society you have Black and North African people who are rich, and you have white people who are poor. I think that the aim of literature is to say reality is complex. But the other thing was what you emphasised – the humiliation of Louise, because she's doing an immigrant's job. When you're white and doing a job that is done, 99 per cent of the time, by immigrants, I think that you feel very humiliated and very lonely.

**AB:** That sensation of loneliness was something that kept coming to me when I was reading the book. Louise is essentially homeless. There's a moment where she says she's haunted by the feeling that she's seen too much, had too much of other people's privacy. This put me in mind of something quite early in the book when Myriam is reflecting on her condition and says, 'We will only be happy when we don't need one another any more, when we can live a life of our own.' Both of them seem to have come to the same conclusion, but with very different results.

**LS:** Yeah. But you know, what is very difficult in the job of a nanny is that you raise children. Sometimes you see them walk for the first time. You love them a lot and you have to leave. Then you do it again and again and again. For me, she is like a lover who has a lot of break-ups. So, of course, she's homeless because she has always lived in other people's homes. Her home is nothing. For Myriam, it's different. When she looks at her children, she has this very weird feeling that I think a lot of parents have: that they depend on you, and that's something beautiful because they love you. But sometimes it's terrible. Sometimes you just want to leave because it's too much. So I wanted to show that being a mother and being needed is not just something wonderful. Sometimes it's something very dark, and very difficult to deal with.

**AB:** I'd like to finish on a question of process. Towards the end we meet this police captain who's about to lead a reconstruction in the flat. She says that she thinks reconstructions are sometimes revelatory, like those voodoo ceremonies where the trance state causes a truth to burst up from the pain, where the past is illuminated in a new light. When I read that, I couldn't help but make the comparison with your task as a novelist.

**LS:** Of course. It's a metaphor for the novelist.

**AB:** Right. And writing a novel is something that one enters into in a physical and emotional way. It can be quite draining and quite exhausting. So I'm curious; once you'd set these characters in motion and got to know them, do you feel, firstly, that you came to understand them? And, secondly, do you think you came to understand why a character, a person, like Louise, could commit the kind of act she did?

**LS:** That's why I decided to write the chapter about the captain. She's actually a metaphor for the writer. What I wanted to express is that you understand some pieces of your character but you don't understand everything. You try to. You try, as she says, to put your hand in the soul of the character. You try to dominate the situation, but you can't, because there's always something that you don't understand, something that is impossible to express. I have some writer friends who told me that sometimes they can't write because they are waiting for their character to come back. I always laughed and thought, 'Well, that's not true.' But actually it is true. I remember this story about Tolstoy when he was writing *Anna Karenina*. His editor had given him a lot of money to write. He was waiting for the manuscript, but nothing was coming. So he went to Tolstoy's house, and he said, 'Give me the book or give me back the money because I'm very tired of waiting.' And Tolstoy looked at him and said, 'Anna Karenina is gone. I'm waiting for her.' And you laugh, but that's true. Sometimes you're just waiting for the character. He comes, you write about him, and then he goes back and you don't really know where he is. It's a mystery.

# Reni Eddo-Lodge

## *Why I'm No Longer Talking to White People About Race*

### Tuesday 3rd April 2018

~

**Adam Biles:** Sometimes a book comes along that manages not just to capture a moment, but to catalyse a movement. *Why I'm No Longer Talking to White People About Race* by Reni Eddo-Lodge is just such a book. An exposition of structural racism and its effects that is both authoritative and personal, *Why I'm No Longer Talking to White People About Race* hasn't so much provoked a debate as performed the long-overdue task of redefining the very terms upon which the debate is conducted. As Reni Eddo-Lodge writes in the preface, 'it's about not just the explicit side, but the slippery side of racism, the bits that are hard to define, and the bits that make you doubt yourself'. It's also about history, systems, privilege, feminism, class and the media. Please welcome Reni Eddo-Lodge to Shakespeare and Company.

**Reni Eddo-Lodge:** Thank you, everybody, for being here today.

**AB:** I'd like to begin tonight with a sentence that came just towards the end of the original blog post that gave rise to this book. You write: 'I don't have a huge amount of power to change the way the world works, but I can set boundaries.' Four years after you wrote that blog post and having seen what it's led on to – with both the writing of the book and the sensation it has become – did you have any idea when you wrote that sentence how powerful the setting of boundaries could be?

**REL:** No. For me, it was a very personal boundary. I'm somebody who's been writing diaries for my entire life, and writing on the internet in blogging form since I was thirteen or something. So, you know, I wrote that on my blog that nobody was reading. And my blog was linked to my Twitter. So when I pressed publish, that also went out on my Twitter. So I was just talking about my personal boundary. But you know what writing's like. It's almost a way of setting your intentions, holding yourself accountable. So that's what I did. It's not that I didn't think anyone was going to read it because, you know, you write on the internet, you hope somebody listens. But I was just blindsided by the amount of people who read it, and who also suggested to me that they were feeling exactly the same way. But it was also something that I felt very much alone in dealing with while I was involved in various activist groups. I would talk about it with them, but we were on the margins. So yeah, I suppose a weird thing about setting that personal boundary was that the opposite has happened. At least I'm now speaking about race on my own terms rather than being dragged into these pointless, destructive, wildly unbalanced conversations where I'm put on the spot and told to justify myself, which I think happens a lot when people try to speak up about racial inequality. The general consensus is that that's not a problem – prove it. So I wrote the book to prove it.

**AB:** One of the ways of speaking about it on your own terms is by concentrating a big chunk of the beginning of the book on history, specifically on the history of Black people in Britain. It becomes very clear very quickly how important understanding that history is to the direction the book is going to take.

**REL:** Context is key. That's what I was finding as an activist and a blogger trying to have these conversations. I'd often get, 'Oh, that's an American problem. We don't really have that here, so I don't know why you're complaining.' But I knew that wasn't the case. It wasn't something I learned on the curriculum at school, but I knew anecdotally from older Black people around me that there had been some serious, serious mistreatment just one generation before I was born. So I made it my mission. Also, I'm a journalist. That's important to mention, because when you're talking about an issue as a journalist you have to provide some big picture analysis about the phenomenon that's happening. So for me it was very important to provide that context. I think something that I came across in activist circles a lot was conversations, particularly from the older generation, about young people of colour not knowing their history, not knowing where they came from blah, blah, blah. Almost the suggestion that it was our responsibility that knowledge wasn't being passed down. But on the curriculum at school I'd only learnt about Martin Luther King and Rosa Parks and things in an American context. So I thought, rather than complaining about us not knowing our history, let me just find it. So I spent a lot of time in the British Library and the Black Cultural Archives in Brixton just going through old books and archived material. And it wasn't hard to find and it wasn't difficult to access. The only issue was that it hadn't been reproduced in the narrative of the country as 'the story of Britain' in the same way that other historical narratives had. And that's why it was written out.

**AB:** Do you think that the reason the British curriculum seems more comfortable talking about, for example, the civil rights movement in the United States rather than Black British history is because if we were to engage with some of the history that you talk about in the book it would pose a lot of difficult questions that people just don't want to face?

**REL:** Well, it would probably prompt too much self-reflection, which Britain doesn't like to do that much. We'd rather just shout about how colonialism was actually amazing. I have not had direct conversations with the people who set Britain's national curriculum, but it seems to me that there's a deep unwillingness. And this gets reproduced generation after generation. It's not like one day somebody knew and then decided not to write it down. One generation of kids doesn't learn it, so they don't know. And then they go off to be teachers and they haven't learnt it, and they teach kids who don't know. So while researching that portion of the book I collated these historical documents, and also got in touch with people who were doing work around civil rights in Britain in the seventies and eighties. A lot of these people are still alive. The documents are very easy to access. It's just never been put in front of people before.

**AB:** One of the people you spoke to was Linda Bellos, who was one of the founders of Black History Month UK. We feel a frustration on her part. She says 'they don't know why we're in this country'. And she goes on to say that for her it was important that it be *History* Month, not *Culture* Month. Which made me think that in Britain people do seem quite comfortable celebrating events like the Notting Hill Carnival and talking about chicken tikka masala as the national dish, but don't seem to have the same willingness to engage with the history that led to these different cultures being present in the UK. Which seems to be kind of a disconnect in the national psyche.

**REL:** In a way, yes. Again, I think it's just a reluctance to prompt any sort of self-reflection, which is a bit weird to me because I think some other countries in the global north are fairly alright at looking at their own histories of discrimination and oppression – Germany, for example. The US is slowly making progress on that front too. At least one half of it is. So it's nice to talk about everyone having fun and eating food and enjoying each other and going to Notting Hill Carnival and there's a white policeman dancing, but there's very little discussion about the struggle that actually led to the Notting Hill Carnival in the first place. I just feel like it's a metaphor for life. You can't just take the good bits without actually looking at the struggle. That's why people have therapists, you know. Because if you try to just ignore and repress the difficult emotions, whether individually or nationally, you're going to have some problems. So, yeah, that was a deep frustration. I think for Linda Bellos as well.

**AB:** I think one of the other reasons that it's vital to know this history is that it can help avoid repeating the same mistakes. So you talk about the case with Robert Relf, who put up a sign saying he would only sell his house to English people . . .

**REL:** By which he meant white people.

**AB:** Yes. And you talk about how this led to a media campaign against political correctness. That this was the seed of this idea that political correctness was in some way ridiculous or in some way destructive. It struck me that there's a similar sort of dynamic going on at the moment with terms like 'intersectionality' or 'safe spaces'. There seems to be a concerted attempt in certain media organisations to undermine these terms. I wonder if people were more familiar with how the media had previously sought to undermine political correctness, whether it would be harder for the same tactics to work again.

**REL:** Yeah, I mean, political correctness is not a phrasing I use, but I looked through the archival material and saw what the papers were actually angry at. They were rallying around a man who was trying to operate a discriminatory housing policy. And the local government said, 'you can't do that' because what he was doing was illegal. I don't understand any media campaign for cruelty between human beings, but I'm not a newspaper editor. I guess I don't understand that the bottom line is to sell papers.

In terms of reckoning with history: if you don't really engage with what happened just one generation previously or even two generations previously, you're doomed to make the same mistakes. In the book I quoted the emeritus director of the Institute of Race Relations in the UK – his name was Ambalavaner Sivanandan – and he said, 'We are here because you were there.' He said that about Britain's immigrant experience. And it's not just immigrants. I really do think that's a lazy term in this context, because we're talking about people who are now second-, and third-generation. These are naturalised British people, including myself. I think that that phrasing – 'we are here because you were there' – is so important. Britain literally went to these countries. Unless there's a widespread understanding of what that means, then you're going to constantly have these conversations about where all these people have come from. In the fifties and sixties, Jamaicans were turning up on British shores because it was the mother country. So it seems absurd just twenty years later how they were being treated by the police, who were acting as an arm of the British state. 'You were there.' I think that's so important. That's a context that I think is not passed down, not taught. It's deeply frustrating. But I hope that more people understand what that's been like. Not just from reading the book, but also in the bibliography. I point towards the UK historian Stephen Bourne. He's a self-taught historian who's done loads of work around this. But I also feel like the onus can't just be on each individual becoming educated. There needs to be more of a widespread understanding of what the 'you were there' actually meant. It means the global north's colonialism project.

**AB:** That brings us quite nicely on to one of the central cruxes of the book: the concept of structural racism. Now you prefer the term 'structural' to 'institutional' because, if I understood correctly, the idea of structure takes in a society beyond specific institutions.

**REL:** Yeah. You know, if it's easier for you to understand 'institutional', fine. But for me, I want to talk about structures, because I think anything can be a structure. There's a family structure. There can be a friendship-group structure. There can be your workplace, small or large. It can also be the National Health Service, the police, the education system. But I don't wish to quibble on that.

**AB:** For anybody in the audience who has not yet read the book, or who might not be quite aware of what structural racism is, would you be able to give us a quick explanation of what you mean by the term?

**REL:** There is a wealth of data about demographics and wealth and opportunity and inequality in Britain, which means it's really easy to look at the numbers and see who's being held back or which groups – and I use that term loosely, because we know that not everybody who shares the same skin colour considers themselves part of a group – are being discriminated against. So I just looked at this data, from umbrella bodies connected to higher education, health care, the criminal justice system, etc., etc. I looked at race and opportunity. And I found repeatedly that if you are not white, your life chances are impeded by that fact. The demographics and the stats in the UK show us that if you are not white you are far more likely to be working class than if you are white. That's not to say that white people are not also living in poverty in Britain. It's just that the working class is overwhelmingly populated by people who are not white. That's also not to say that there is not a thriving Black middle class. It's just far smaller.

So I found stats that basically showed that Black boys were far more likely to be excluded from school in the primary school system than their white counterparts. When it came to eleven-year-olds taking their exams to get into secondary school, Black children were being under-marked by their own teachers in those exams. That was actually something that was rectified by anonymous marking. When it came to higher education, I found that Black students were far more likely to get a lower grade than their white counterparts. Then, when you leave university – according to a report done by the government's Department for Work and Pensions in 2009 – people with African and Asian sounding names applying for jobs alongside people with white British sounding names, with similar qualifications and experience, were far less likely to be called to a job interview. I kept finding, when looking at the data, that if you were not white – or sometimes even perceived to be not white, in terms of your name – then your life chances were impeded. So I thought there has to be one of two explanations for this. It's either that these people whose life chances are impeded are just inherently inferior, and that's why they're being discriminated against at every point. Or there is some broad discrimination happening here. And I don't think it's as simple as saying it's KKK members reading the CVs. It's not actually an overt-hatred type of racism. But there's clearly some bias there. And that's what I meant, really, by structural racism.

**AB:** This, in a way, goes radically against the story Britain has been telling itself, at least over the last thirty or forty years, of essentially being a meritocracy. But people who subscribe to the meritocracy idea can't, essentially, accept the structural idea because one would completely undermine the other.

**REL:** You know, I'm now doing a veritably middle-class profession. I know lots of people of colour in middle-class professions who are excellent at what they do, but they still feel like they probably would have gone further if their name didn't look a little bit foreign on their CV. Concerning meritocracy – yes, of course hard work matters. I'm not saying here that because of structural racism hard work doesn't matter. But the injustice is that people work hard, and yet there are external factors impeding their potential and their progress. That's what I'm annoyed about. One of the refrains you'll always get from those who are seeking to downplay the problem is: 'You want unqualified people. You want a quota and those people won't be qualified for the job.' But I know so many people, particularly in the creative industries, who are wildly qualified and not getting the opportunities that they deserve. The issue here is that if you are discriminating – consciously or unconsciously – on race, you're actually allowing some mediocrity into the net. I look at Britain's creative and political industries, and I look at the people who hold positions of power in Britain, and I see that they're all white, male and middle-aged. And I just don't believe that the only people who are talented in that country are white, male or middle-aged. I refuse to believe it. I know it's not true.

**AB:** You cite a study on racial prejudice at the top level of British business in which the statistics basically say it's almost exclusively white, male, middle-aged. And this guy says, 'Oh, there's little sign of systemic racial prejudice at the top of British business. We've investigated and there's little sign of it.' There seems to be a level of cognitive dissonance. 'Statistically our employees are in no way representative of British society, but we've done our study and we can't find any prejudice.'

**REL:** It's frustrating for me as a writer and a journalist because I studied my English literature, I read the canon, I paid attention to every philosopher. And I would say that white men have often been seen as the arbiters of logical, rational thinking. OK, cool. But then there were instances like the one you've just mentioned, in which one of these supposed arbiters can't see the wood for the trees. And that's frustrating because I'm a journalist; I love objectivity, I love to look for the truth. It's frustrating for me where you can see somebody's bias creeping in, which is actually stopping them from reaching the conclusion that the evidence shows them. As an activist, I was always put in the position where I had to provide evidence. Which is part of the reason I became a journalist. So I did that. It's frustrating that there are still some people who refuse to look at that evidence.

**AB:** But because of the way that British society has been structured for so long, there has been no need for white people generally, and probably white men in particular, to recognise this.

**REL:** There's also a point in the book where I talk about a real disparity that I know, at least anecdotally, to be true. When I was growing up in South London, I was told by my mum, 'Look, you're always going to have to work twice as hard as your white counterparts if you want to get on in life.' And meanwhile, my white friends were being told by their parents, 'Everyone's equal, everyone's the same, it's fine.' So we've got two different messages there, and that's very concerning.

**AB:** You talk about this idea of colour-blindness. I think I was brought up with this idea, and I think my parents were probably very well-meaning in doing so. But you have a very interesting perspective on that. That it's not useful. In fact, it's in some way going to be an impediment to a just society.

**REL:** Yes, of course. I think that if you believe in fair play, then why would you not basically base your stance on this, on the evidence and then work towards a position that is fair? You know, I'm not anti-meritocracy. I love the idea of meritocracy. That's why I'm an anti-racist, because I see that it's a point in the future we need to get to. But unless we deal with discrimination, we're not going to get there. For me the idea of collecting the evidence and the data was so important. So it's very interesting to be speaking in a country where collecting the evidence and the data is literally illegal. [A French law, dating from 1978, bans the collection of personal data based on race, ethnicity, political, religious or philosophical opinion, trade union associations, health or sex life.] I don't know, am I going to get arrested when I leave? So yeah, I wholeheartedly believe in fair play. I think everybody should have the potential to start on a level playing field. But the evidence shows that we're not there. We are not there yet. So let's just be honest about it. We're not perfect as individuals or as nation states, so why lie about it?

**AB:** In the new chapter – 'Aftermath' – you write about giving a talk at a school and somebody in the audience, a white lady, asking 'what's the end point?' And the young lady afterwards saying she thinks people who are looking for an end point are refusing to recognise the complexity and the difficulty of the situation. They just kind of want rid of it, in fact. And that's the thing: this is not a book of easy solutions.

**REL:** People love to ask me for easy solutions. So don't do that today because I will not answer your question!

**AB:** There are not many surreal moments in this book, but one is where you interview Nick Griffin, the leader of the British National Party, which was essentially the British National Front. It's quite an experience, as a reader, running up against his words in the middle of yours. Could you just talk a little bit about why you decided to include this interview and what the experience was actually like for you.

**REL:** Well, I was writing about him and his political ideology from about ten years earlier, and then my editor said I should probably just get in touch with him to make sure that what I was saying was correct, because we don't want to get sued. So I said, 'OK, I'll do that.' I was able to get in touch with him because one of the editors I worked with in a journalistic capacity had written a book about the BNP a few years back. So I just wrote to him. The conversation was so weird, but also I felt that it needed to go into the book in full, somewhat consciously contradicting the title. I also think that with some narratives that were happening around Brexit and Trump – about what I call in the book 'a fear of a black planet', demographic change and that kind of stuff – I just wanted to remind people where those ideas came from. All the news coverage, particularly around Trump's election, was of how a certain demographic called the 'white working class' are scared of demographic change and being under threat. I should say I believe this is a fallacious demographic, because the evidence shows that the working class is as much brown and black as it is white. But that was being parroted on national news channels as a reason why Trump was elected. So my conversation with Nick Griffin really did just get us back to the origins of that narrative. I just want people to remember what they're parroting when they're saying that.

**AB:** That phrase 'white working class' is a very curious thing. I remember growing up in Britain in the eighties and nineties, when class was the last thing you were allowed to talk about. This was a moment when you had a Labour leader who had been very expensively privately educated, and if you brought up class, you were told, 'How dare you? How could you say that just because someone's incredibly rich, he can't understand the problems on a council estate . . .'

**REL:** He can't! Being incredibly rich, how can he?

**AB:** Right! And yet fascinatingly, over the last few years, as you point out, when it comes to playing this new game of divide and rule, essentially when it is suddenly useful for the political class to talk about this concept of the working class again, suddenly it becomes a sort of a political buzzword and it's OK.

**REL:** Of course. I think that where Britain gained in conversations about race in the mid-nineties – around the time of the Stephen Lawrence inquiry and the Macpherson report and all of that stuff . . . what it lacked was really just stating the truth. Which is that this is an issue of race and class. So there have supposedly been anti-racist narratives that have left class out of the equation, which I just don't think is sufficient enough. And that's why there's a whole chapter in the book about race and class and housing, in particular in the London borough that I grew up in, Tottenham and Haringey. It just gives you an idea of who's actually losing out, who is literally on the ground losing out from the class narrative. One thing I say in the book is that we've got this conception of a working-class person being, you know, a stocky northern white man in a flat cap. When actually I think it's closer to a Black woman in London, a single mum pushing a buggy. That's what the evidence shows us. So we can't not integrate those things. They are not one and the same, but they're so closely intertwined.

**AB:** And the other big chapter towards the end, which comes before the one on class, is the chapter on feminism. I thought it was fascinating the way you construct your argument throughout the book, because it becomes very clear that you cannot really be a feminist if you're not anti-racist. You can't be a class warrior if you're not anti-racist. You can't be anti-racist if you're not also a feminist and a class warrior. These are all inseparable concepts.

**REL:** Yes, indeed. And I think that each movement fails when it doesn't take those things into account. My chapter on feminism was actually the first chapter I wrote. I don't know if anybody can tell, but I was pretty annoyed. I think that the feminist movement in Britain, between 2012 and 2015, made some wins. But for whom? I mean, OK, we've got some fairly thoughtful media representations of white, middle-class, slim ladies. But, I don't know. I just feel like that's not exciting. So, yeah, we still really need some progress on that front.

# Jesmyn Ward

## *Sing, Unburied, Sing*

Thursday 26th April 2018

~

**Adam Biles:** *Sing, Unburied, Sing* begins with death in all its stench and slime and bloody viscera. It's an aroma that hangs in the air, and one that Jesmyn Ward never fully allows to lift as she leads readers into her exquisitely written third novel. Our guides are Jojo – on the cusp of adulthood and beset with all the uncertainties that entails, particularly for a young African American – Jojo's mother, Leonie; and a third voice so striking and unconventional that I'll let Jesmyn decide whether and how we talk about it this evening. *Sing, Unburied, Sing* drives us through the torrid Mississippi countryside, but also traverses the potholed political landscape of contemporary America, engaging with questions of racism, of poverty, of incarceration, of drug addiction, and the point at which they explosively intersect.

Jesmyn Ward is the first female author to win two National Book Awards for Fiction, for *Salvage the Bones* in 2011 and last year, of course, for *Sing, Unburied, Sing*. Please join me in welcoming Jesmyn Ward to Shakespeare and Company.

**Jesmyn Ward:** Thank you so much.

108

**AB:** The opening to the book sets the tone of what we're to expect. It's also a very bold opening. You ask a lot of your reader by confronting them not just with the concept of death, but with very vivid descriptions of what death involves. In this case it's a goat that has died, but it's not much of a mental leap to project that onto humans. Why did you decide to begin the book with such a bold image?

**JW:** I always like to begin with a strong image in the same way that I like to end with a strong image. The very beginning has to do so much right. It has to make the reader want to continue reading. It has to hook the reader, but it also has to give some indication of what the driving force, or the driving theme behind the book is. I knew this would be a book about death, from the very beginning of the rough draft. That's why I decided I wanted to open with the death. I was also thinking about *Salvage the Bones*, my second novel, about the way that novel opened with life, with birth. So I thought, OK, because I'm writing about death and because I've already written about birth, it's right for me to start with the slaughter of this animal that's going to feed this family. You know, Jojo is a very deprived child in many respects. The death of the goat is this moment of great violence. But what is behind that violence is a certain tenderness and a certain kindness and a certain caring. That slaughter is almost an expression of love from Pop for his grandson.

**AB:** Because it's Jojo's birthday, and because he's at the very precise age of thirteen, it also feels like a rite of passage, the beginning of his transition into adulthood. So most of the book is told either from the perspective of Jojo or Leonie, and this third voice. When you conceived of this family and the story you wanted to tell, was it always obvious to you which voices you would tell it through?

**JW:** I found Jojo first. When I was casting about for novel ideas, he popped into my head. He was a thirteen-year-old mixed-race boy growing up in very difficult circumstances. And that was true of him from the beginning. I wasn't sure what the specifics would be, but I knew that he was going through a rough time, and that he was, in some respects, a child being made to bear adult burdens. I just wasn't sure what exactly those burdens would be. So I knew that his voice was important from the very beginning. But I did want other characters to be able to narrate their own sections at first. I thought, well, maybe I'll have three or four or five, but I decided that I should focus, and that the other first-person point of view should be his mother's. It took me a while to figure out who Leonie was as a character. At first I didn't realise she was Black. I thought she would be white. At first I thought that Jojo would have multiple siblings, so she would have multiple children. And she wasn't always struggling with addiction. She wasn't always as abusive as she is in the book. But I had to figure out some of that before I began. Then I learned more about her as I went. Then you have Richie, the ghost. I didn't actually commit to writing chapters from his perspective until somewhere between the thirteenth and fifteenth revision, and only at the suggestion of my editor. I thought about it when I discovered Richie as a character, but I think I was afraid to do so. So when my editor asked that it was as if it was a vote of confidence from her. So I tried it.

**AB:** Resting with Jojo for a moment, you said he came to you first, and you knew he was a young mixed-race boy in a difficult situation. Was the emergence of Jojo as a character connected to the increasing news stories about young Black boys, for example, being shot by police, and, more broadly, the discriminatory treatment in their lives?

**JW:** I don't know if his character came to me for those reasons necessarily. I've been writing about younger characters for a while in my fiction. So I don't know if there's a direct correlation between the two. I do know that I was very aware of all the Black men and Black women and Black children that were being killed while I was sort of casting about for ideas. When I wanted to begin writing this book, I think that's one of the reasons why I knew from the very beginning that a policeman would show up sometime during the story and there'd be a very tense moment.

**AB:** We'll certainly come on to that a little bit later. Concerning this idea of writing about younger characters – while Jojo is on the cusp of turning into an adult, Leonie is an adult. But at the same time, there's something almost childlike about her, or certainly immature.

**JW:** Leonie's somewhere in her mid-twenties – I am horrible at math, so I can't tell you off the top of my head exactly how old she is. But I worked it out while I was writing the book. I think part of the reason that readers might get that impression of Leonie, and I think that it's a totally legitimate impression, is because she's carrying so many traumas from her childhood and from her adolescence with her as an adult. She hasn't figured out how to live with them as a healthy adult. And this affects her behaviour with her parents, with her children, with her struggle with addiction. Her grief at losing her brother, her belief that she has continuously disappointed her parents with the private decisions that she's made in her life. I think that she can't sit with the pain of those things, so can't figure out how to live with them in a healthy way as an adult. So she's really stuck.

**AB:** In a book that is determined to engage with the subject of death, I suppose there's an inevitability that ghosts will be a part of that. But what form those ghosts take could be varied. There's ghosts as a sort of metaphor, or as visions. And then there are ghosts that have a real literal existence in the plot. One of the things you do so brilliantly in *Sing, Unburied, Sing* is play with these different distinctions. So here we have Leonie, who sees her brother as part of what might be dismissed as a drug-induced vision. And yet, as the book progresses, we realise that the ghosts are much more present and much more real than that.

**JW:** I really wasn't committed to writing a ghost story when I began *Sing, Unburied, Sing*. I knew there would be an element of magical realism to this story. I knew that Jojo could look at animals and understand what they were trying to communicate to him. I knew that Leonie was seeing a phantom. But in the first draft, she was actually seeing a phantom of Michael, she wasn't seeing a phantom of her brother. One of the things that I knew at the very beginning of the rough draft was that these characters were heading to Parchman Prison to pick Michael up. But I knew nothing about Parchman Prison. So I started doing research. Parchman Prison farm is in the Delta, in Mississippi state. I think it's the biggest prison in Mississippi. It was the first big state prison in Mississippi. And it has a really horrible, violent history. It was only established sometime during the late 1800s, early 1900s, but once the prison was built, the lawmakers in this state decided to actually change the laws so that things like loitering was criminalised. They knew that they could get a large population of Black male inmates by tailoring these laws so that these were the people they could stock the prison with. In the beginning, they rented these men and boys out to industrial barons in the region. The men and boys laid tracks for railroads. They would clear vast tracts of forests while they were chained to each other. Then, somewhere around the thirties, they decided that Parchman Prison basically would be a working plantation. And that's what they made it into. The inmates were made to work in the fields before dawn, throughout the day, and then only ended after dusk. If they did not harvest quickly enough they were whipped with the whip called Black Betty. They were sometimes killed. If they tried to escape, they were hunted with dogs. Some of the inmates were actually made into guards. These guards would stand at the edges of the fields and they would watch the inmates as they were working in the fields. And if one of the inmates tried to escape and one of these inmate guards shot the inmate who was trying to escape, then that inmate guard would be set free. It didn't matter what he'd done to end up in Parchman, but he would be set free. So I learned all that. And then I learned that Black boys as young as twelve were charged with things like loitering and were sent to Parchman Prison. As soon as I found out that children like that existed, and that I knew nothing about them, and that their lives and their pain had been basically erased from history, I knew that I had to write about a character like that, like Richie. But I wanted that character to have the agency that he was denied during his life. I wanted him to be able to interact with Jojo, to interact with all the characters in the present. The only way I could accomplish that was by making him into a ghost. So that's how a ghost became a major character in my book. Once I realised Richie was a ghost, I thought back to this phantom that Leonie was seeing. And I thought, 'Well, that phantom Michael is not doing any work in the narrative, so he might as well be a ghost, too.' So it was really the horrific things that I learned about Mississippi and Parchman Prison that made me feel compelled to create these ghosts.

**AB:** Another thing that using ghosts in a narrative allows you to do is to give this sense of a collapse of time, and to overlap layers of history and draw parallels between the way things are now and the way things were in Richie's day and earlier – Richie also seemed to connect to the oral storytelling tradition, which is itself connected to first-person narratives. Could you talk a little bit about your approach to history, to oral storytelling, and reflect on why this book had to be written in first-person narratives?

**JW:** Writing in the first person is easier for me. I think one of the reasons it's easier is because when I write in the third person I'm just very conscious of the fact that I am making all the choices. It makes the process of writing more tortured. It also makes that process go very slowly, because I'm constantly second-guessing every line, every word, every bit of punctuation, because I'm so self-conscious about that. I am doing this, I'm creating this. I think it makes my writing weaker because there's a certain distance. Once I wrote my first short story in the first person I thought, 'Oh, this is great. I'm staying right here.' It just felt more natural to me. It felt as if these characters whose voices I was inhabiting were right here and they were talking to me, and I was listening and just channelling them. So it felt a bit more effortless. I was less aware of myself. I also think that there's value in having characters speak from a first-person point of view, especially when you're writing about people who have traditionally been silent first. The kind of people that I write about have traditionally been silenced. Their voices have not been a part of the narrative in the United States. Whether I'm writing from the perspective of a fifteen-year-old pregnant, Black, poor teenager in *Salvage the Bones*, or if I'm writing from that of a drug-addicted abusive twenty-something-year-old mother who neglects her children, or if I am writing about a thirteen-year-old boy who's trying to understand what it means to be a man and what it means to be a human being in the modern South.

**AB:** There are a lot of themes in *Sing, Unburied, Sing*: incarceration, drug addiction, racism. And one way to look at it is as a 'state of the nation' novel, or at least a state of a particular part of the nation. But as I was reading, I realised that when you're in a situation of poverty these are just the kind of problems that intersect over you.

**JW:** True. I write about the kind of people who are members of my family. I write about the kind of people who are members of my community. I'm from this small town on the coast of Mississippi. This small, poor community on the coast of Mississippi. So I see the effects of generational poverty all around me. I see many people in my community, many people in my family, struggling with drug addiction. Since I am choosing to write about the people that I write about, I have to be honest about the circumstances of their lives. I also think that, unfortunately, we're at this moment right now in the United States where a narrative is being pushed that the past does not matter and does not bear on the present. We're all equal. And all of these injustices that you perceive are figments of your imagination. In my research I'm learning more about the history of the United States, the history of the South, about slavery and Jim Crow and lynching. The more that I read, the more that I learn that the past is the present, and that the past bears on the present very heavily, in larger systemic ways, but also in very intimate personal ways for many people. So I find myself returning to that idea again and again in my work.

**AB:** There's one moment in which a character talks about pulling all of the weight of history behind him. Part of this narrative you talk about is perpetuated by people who are not obliged to drag the weight of history behind them. We feel this very strongly in the scene with the police officer. It's certainly one of the most tense scenes in the book, in a very physically affecting way.

**JW:** Yeah. As I said before, I felt I knew that it had to happen in the book because it seemed true to when I thought about who my characters were, where they were from, when I thought about the place that shaped them. It had to happen. It was difficult to write. It was interesting because I don't plot everything out when I write. I don't know if I've communicated that to you yet, but I don't plot everything out. I just go with the story. I go with the characters and sometimes they do things that surprise me. Sometimes events happen that I do not expect. So in that moment, it felt like the kind of moment where anything could happen. I had to do something that was very tricky, which was making sure that the love that I feel for Jojo as a character and the sympathy that I feel for him – and the protectiveness that I feel for him – didn't get in the way of what was in that scene.

**AB:** When I was reading it, I was thinking of how in recent years the image of the flashing blue light is no longer a reassuring image – even to those to whom it once was. The experience of African Americans particularly with police has become much more a part of the public consciousness. And this has revealed a whole wealth of experience, which again was prevented from being told.

**JW:** Yeah, definitely. The question is whether or not anything will change now, right? I think that there are tonnes of artists and community activists, and even some lawmakers and politicians, who would like to see that change. But I don't know if it will. I hope it will. It would be nice to not feel as if your life is in danger every time you encounter the police. It would also be nice to not feel policed all the time. There have been times during my life where sometimes the police are just very overbearing. They pull people over just to pull them over. Then when people resist, when they want to know why they've been pulled over, they threaten to arrest them. Sometimes they do arrest them. They're arresting fifty-year-old mothers and their thirty-year-old daughters. It makes you feel as if you are living in a police state and as if you don't have rights. Living with that, day in and day out, is very traumatic.

**AB:** There's a moment where Jojo reflects, 'There's no happiness here'. It's true that in that family there's a lot to be unhappy about. There's also a lot of love in that family. One of the many things I think is admirable about the book is that as it draws to a conclusion you don't reach for an easy sense of hope, or any easy conclusions. And yet, at the same time, I have a certain confidence in Jojo. That if Jojo was left to his own devices, that's where the hope might lie. Is that something that you feel about him too?

**JW:** Yes, I do. I feel that about Jojo and about Michaela. Part of the reason that I feel that is because I know that they have a reserve of love and caring and kindness to draw on that was given to them by Pop and by Mam. I think that those relationships between the grandparents, the love that they share between the grandparents and grandchildren, between the siblings, I think that is sort of shoring them up so that when they go out in a world that continuously tries beat them down, that . . . they'll be able to bear up underneath the things that they must survive because they'll have that to draw on. I know that my endings are not happy or hopeful in an easy way. But I do feel like they're hopeful. Something that I've been thinking about a lot lately is trauma. When I write characters like Pop and Jojo and Kayla and Mam and even Richie and Leonie, I feel like it's important for me to develop them as well as I can, to make them as complicated and as human as I can on the page, because I believe that we are more than our trauma. In the wider conversation, in the media and in some books in the past, we've been reduced to our trauma again and again and again. I think that makes it harder for people outside of our communities to see us as fully concrete, complicated human beings. So I feel like it's part of my job to write in a way that the reader understands that fact, and understands we're more than our trauma, and understands that we experience joy and exhibit tenderness and exhibit kindness just like any other human being would.

# Carlo Rovelli

## The Order of Time

Wednesday 13th June 2018

~

**Adam Biles:** Why do we remember the past and not the future? Do we exist in time or does time exist in us? What does it really mean to say that time passes? What ties time to our subjectivity? Professor Carlo Rovelli asks all of these questions in his latest book, *The Order of Time*, and then takes readers on a journey that doesn't just seek to address them, but to churn up the apparently firm foundations from which they were posed. It's often dizzying, frequently unsettling, and yet also a transcendent reading experience. Professor Rovelli takes deeply complex, often counterintuitive scientific ideas, concepts of quantum gravity and indeterminacy, and renders them understandable to – well, let's be frank – to someone like me. To pull all this off, he calls upon his extensive literary gifts, his profoundly subtle and supple mind, but also the words of Shakespeare, and even the Grateful Dead. The result is a book that is as philosophical as it is scientific, as concerned with the nuances of abstract theories as it is with the beauty of humanistic thought. Please join me in welcoming Carlo Rovelli to Shakespeare and Company.

**Carlo Rovelli:** Thank you very much. It's such a joy being in this place. This place is magic. The possibility of spending two days here, living upstairs, is wonderful. You couldn't be in a better place in Paris.

**AB:** I'd like to begin with talking about the notion of time itself, with how we experience it. It's something which has been very difficult for us to pin down. Why is this?

**CR:** The main point is that time is a very complex notion, with many sides, many aspects. Some of these are obvious and essential to us. We couldn't even imagine ourselves without time. We think we know what time is; we have the idea times flows from the past to the present to the future. We imagine time as a long line, like a thread. It passes. The future is intrinsically different from the present. Now we are in the present. The current present in London is the same as here. The present in New York is the same. The present all over the universe is the same present. Time is measured by watches, and all watches move at the same speed . . .

Well, almost everything I just said is wrong. It's wrong in the sense that it describes an approximation to a more complex structure. But let me immediately add one thing: time for us is more than what I said. It's not just the clock time that passes, the time we use to organise our lives. It's also something with a strong emotional side. There are times when it feels like its sliding away, when we don't have time. It's connected to our memories, our joys, our sorrows, and our desire that things happen; our entire emotional life is attached to such sliding time. It is complicated for us to disentangle all this, because of all the different layers that make up our notion of time.

**AB:** There's something quite contradictory about the way we think of it. So you mentioned clock time. I think that would be broadly the way most of us would think of time. We think it's more or less the same for everybody. And yet even from personal experience we know this isn't the case. There's a line in Barthes's *A Lover's Discourse* when he talks about how waiting for a phone call feels much longer than it does to the person who is waiting to make the phone call.

**CR:** I remember that from high school . . . girls saying they would call me . . .

**AB:** Exactly, me too! And in a similar vein you talk about how it only takes a few micrograms of LSD to completely change the way we experience time. Yet despite all of this we still tend to think of it as something quite strictly regulated by clocks.

**CR:** In physics we learn that time is flexible, that clocks go at different speeds depending on where you are. We know today people can age at different rates if they are at different altitudes. There's a movie where the hero comes back from an interstellar trip and meets his daughter, who in the meanwhile has become older than him. We know that this is possible. It's not Hollywood fantasy, it's how the world really works. Why then do we wrongly believe that time passes at the same speed for everyone? In our experience of time there's nothing regular. Time sometimes passes fast, sometimes slowly. The idea of regular time is not only wrong physics, but it doesn't match our experience either. The shared and universal clock time is a common idea, but it's not really what we call time. What we call time is a different experience.

The idea that our lives are regulated by clock time is a recent idea, historically. For most of our history clocks didn't exist. A few centuries ago clocks became more common, when churches built clock towers. Up to that point time was basically day and night. The division of the day into twenty-four hours is ancient; it happened 3,000, maybe 4,000 years ago in Mesopotamia. But the division was twelve hours between sunrise and sunset, which meant that in summer an hour was longer than in winter. So for many centuries an hour was a flexible notion. Today we're used to time zones – so Paris and Marseilles have the same time. But this only happened at the end of nineteenth century. Up to that point every little town had its own clock, which was set to midday when the sun was at its zenith. But when the sun is at its zenith in Paris, it is not so in Bordeaux. So Bordeaux was always fifteen minutes after Paris.

This changed only with trains and with the telegraph. Because, of course, if you want to make a timetable it's not easy if every station in the country has a different clock time. It becomes a nightmare. So this idea took hold, that we should all agree on some common time. The Americans proposed a single time for the whole planet. People disliked that, because we're used to the fact that you wake up at eight a.m. and not at five in the afternoon. There was a great debate on how to standardise clock time. And finally a compromise was found: to divide the earth into time zones. The problem then became regulating the clocks on the same time, which is not easy. You have to find a good way. So there were all these strategies for synchronising clocks. And there was a guy in Switzerland who was in a patent office, who was evaluating patents for synchronising clocks. His name was Albert Einstein. This obviously had an effect on him, because at the moment humanity decided to synchronise their clocks Einstein realised that this is impossible because clocks actually tick at different speeds.

**AB:** Which brings us on very nicely to my next question. The social history of how we experience time is something I think everyone here could easily identify with from their personal experience. What you bring to writing about time is a career dedicated, at least in part, to investigating time in science. When you decided to write this book, was it quite a scary prospect, bringing these two vastly different ways of looking at time together and then presenting them in a way that the readers could hopefully understand?

**CR:** The scary part was to talk about a problem which is still open, and which has so many sides to it. I had published *Seven Brief Lessons on Physics*, and a lot of people said that they wanted to read more. I did not want to repeat myself. So I decided to talk about the core of what has fascinated me in science. Time has been the central fascination of my life. It's an incredible subject because we have discovered so much about how time really works which is so different from our everyday experience. But that's one part of the story – to show people that time is not what most people think it is, that there's no time at the fundamental level. The other part of the story is that there's so much we still don't understand about time. There is still a mysterious aspect to it. I wanted to tell the full story. To tell everything we do understand about time, without hiding what we don't understand about it.

**AB:** And indeed there's a turning point in the book, where you write that so far you have told us what is broadly understood. And then you say, 'now some of the things I'm going to present are less sure, but they are what my instinct tells me'. This gives the book essentially a kind of classic three act structure, with time as its hero. So in part one we discover everything we thought we knew was wrong. Then we have this descent into an abyss, which you describe as this empty, windswept landscape where all our preconceptions have been stripped away, and we have to figure out how deal with it. And then in part three it's the return to the hearth, in which you return to the human experience and help us digest everything we've learnt, and figure out how that might relate to our experience. Was that a journey that you felt that you had gone on yourself when you first started studying?

**CR:** Yes, it's partially reflecting my own experience, because all my research about quantum gravity takes place without time. We go farther and farther away into the desert, into the wilderness, into the high mountains. But then the question is: all right, so there's no time in the fundamental structure of the world – what is time for us then? What is this thing that we experience as time? So it was the way the book was conceived, but it's also the quintessential narrative, at least since Gilgamesh.

**AB:** In the first act of the book, you compare the discoveries about time to children getting older and discovering that the world is not exactly how it was within the four walls in which they grew up. As if, as a species, we've been going through the same process, which started with the Greek scientist Anaximander – who gives us the title of the book – who was, in a sense, the first scientist as we understand the term.

**CR:** Yes. I think that science is, largely, a collective way of learning. Similar to the way in which we grow up from childhood. First we think there's only Paris. Then we realise there's France too. And then we realise that the world is not just France, it's Europe. And so on and so forth. And so science is strongly cumulative, in spite of much modern philosophy of science saying otherwise. The earth is round. We have learned that. It's with us forever. We keep learning things, and we're surprised – but the surprise is not about how the world is. The surprise is about how blind we were. The discovery is always to discover that our perspective was partial.

Science is under attack today by many sides, and I think this is a problem. It's a danger for society. We're going to weaken one of our best tools. But, of course, science itself has faults. One of the faults is its strong desire to be fully objective. It tends to distance itself from being human. What we need is not just to learn something objectively, we also need a comprehensive structuring in which our scientific knowledge, our human emotions, our sense of why we are alive, hang together in a story, in a narration and a symbol, which may evolve, but which has to integrate our lives. This is what I try to do in the book.

**AB:** Do you think part of the reason science is under attack today is because of the incredible and dizzying advances since Einstein? Is there something unsettling about these concepts like, for example, the nonexistence of the flow of time, that provokes a defensive reaction?

**CR:** I don't think that's why science is under attack, because people who attack science don't even bother about that. Once you start looking into the wonders that we have discovered about the world you're just fascinated because it's beautiful, as strange as magic. It's hard to be against opening your eyes. It's like somebody opens a window and you say, 'I'm against it now'. You're not against it. You might even use the window. Look outside, at the sea, at the eagles. I think science is under attack for different reasons right now, which have to do with the fact that we humans keep fighting with one another and prefer not to listen to good reason. Science is also under attack because of the atomic bomb, because the modern world – which exists largely thanks to science – has come with a lot of great things, but also with a lot of problems, injustices, inequalities. People react against science because they react politically, for concrete reasons.

**AB:** One of the things the book does very successfully is convey a sense of the awe that you feel in practising your work. You spoke a moment ago about the perceived coldness of science. If that is the impression people have, maybe that's why they find it easier to attack it, or at least easier not to defend it. Whereas when reading *The Order of Time*, we get a sense of the absolute wonder that you feel in discovering these things about the universe. If more people could feel that and identify with that, perhaps people would be more likely to rally to the defence of science.

**CR:** Yeah. I fell in love with physics late, but it definitely was a moment when I thought, 'Wow, this is great, this is fantastic, there's so much to learn.' It's beautiful to discover that the world is not as simple as we thought. It's richer. I started writing late, but my writing is a lot about telling my love story with science, placing science and my emotions side by side.

**AB:** For example, in addition to the posters of rock bands that you had on your wall when you were studying you also had a sign with '$10^{-33}$' written on it. Although perhaps you'd better explain . . .

**CR:** Yeah, that's when I fell in love with the issue that has been my main concern for the rest of my life. So, we have discovered that things are made with atoms, right? The calm water in this glass is really zillions of small zigzagging atoms. It was discovered by Boltzmann and all those people at the end of the nineteenth century. But there is a much, much smaller scale where interesting things happen. A much, much, much, much smaller scale. At that scale, space itself has a sort of atomic structure, which we haven't fully figured out yet. That's what I discovered when I was twenty-four, at university. So we actually don't know what space is, what the structure of space is, or the structure of time that comes with it. Discovering this open question was fantastic for me. There's an open problem there, which has to do with a very minimal structure of reality. It's up there to be grabbed. I mean, it's not going to be me alone, but me and my friends, together. We can do it. So I decided that I wanted to do that in life. The scale at which this happens is $10^{-33}$cm. Which is what? 1 billion, billion, billion billionth of a centimetre. Something like that. And so I posted this number on the wall of my room, and said, 'That's where I want to go.'

**AB:** Now, we're not going to be able to do the science justice in the time we have tonight. But I would like to touch on it, because I know there are people who would be interested just to hear about the process that we go through. So in the first part of the book, you've already said that we discover things like time moves differently, time goes at different speeds depending on the height you are . . .

**CR:** That's the first big surprise!

**AB:** And you also talk about the loss of direction . . .

**CR:** Right. That's the second big surprise. In the equation that gives the working of the world, there is no difference between the past and the future. This opens the question: why then, in our experience, is the past so different from the future? Why do we remember the past and we don't remember the future? It's a beautiful question to which we don't yet have a really convincing answer. We understand a lot about it. We understand that it depends on entropy, but it's not over yet. So that's the second thing. There's no distinction between past and future in the working of the universe.

The third discovery is the most hallucinogenic. It's something again that we know well. It's fully established science, but not yet digested by everybody, I would say. It's the fact that the notion of 'now', the present, does not make sense at large distances. 'Now' is only local. We say that you and I are in the same 'now' here, because you look at me, I look at you. And we see each other in the same present. But consider the time that light takes to go from you to me, and from me to you. It is small – it's a fraction of a nanosecond – so we can ignore it. So, I see you in the present because the discrepancy between my present and what I see about you is negligible. But if we want to be precise, I don't see you in the present. I see you how you were a nanosecond ago. So we are never really together. But of course you are close enough, so it doesn't matter. But say you were on Saturn. I would see you as you were two hours ago, and you'd see me two hours ago for you. Say I'd asked the question 'what are you doing right now?' This 'right now' – there is no way to make it precise. There is no sense of the 'now' for faraway things. The 'now' is a notion that comes from disregarding the time it takes light to travel. With our brains we resolve maybe a tenth of a second. In one hundredth of a second light travels further distances than the size of the earth. So we can think of the earth as a whole within a single 'now'. But not the moon. Not Mars. And even much less a faraway galaxy. It takes light six million years to go a faraway galaxy. Therefore 'now' is only here. There is no common 'now' in the universe. This is very strange, isn't it? Because we have been told that reality exists 'now' and that the past doesn't exist any more. So what does it mean to exist if the 'now' is broken in this way?

**AB:** And indeed, you write about the imprecision of the way we experience things. You mentioned 'the blurring' – which is going to become an important concept not just in the way we experience time, but also *why* we experience time.

**CR:** The blurring was crucial in the work of Boltzmann. It was crucial in the work of the guys who have understood thermodynamics – it is connected to why temperature loss is irreversible. These facts and notions are all understood in terms of blurring. One thing I try to do in the book is to make progress with the question of why is the past different from the future. I suggest it's a perspectival fact. It depends on the way we see the world in an imprecise way. It depends on us, not just on the world by itself.

**AB:** So in a sense this idea of the flow of time is more to do with our imprecise tools of perception.

**CR:** Exactly. The flow of time is not in the thing itself, not in the grammar of things. It has to do with the way we, as pieces of nature, interact with the rest. This sense of flowing that we have. It has a lot to do with the fact that our brain works in a certain manner. We have memories of the past. We calculate the future. When we think about time, we are not really thinking about how things correlated to the position of a watch – we are thinking about what is in our brain as memories and anticipation. That's why time is multilayered. It goes from thermodynamics, to relativity, to quantum mechanics, but then it also goes to the structure of the brain and to our emotional reaction to that.

**AB:** As a reader just grappling with these very unusual concepts, this is when we get a sense of reconciliation. When we're on that windswept tundra where we have been told that everything we thought we knew is not the case we could be forgiven for thinking, 'Well, OK, so my experience of the universe is therefore inherently false. What can I rely on?' But that's not actually what you're saying.

**CR:** Yes, that's not at all what I am saying. The book goes to a desolate land – which may be beautiful, but is also inhuman – but then comes back to us. Because the universe we inhabit is our universe. Our view of the universe is not false, but it's our perspective on it. The things that make us are one aspect of the universe. Maybe it's not the fundamental grammar of things, but it's not an illusion either. Our perception is the correct perception from our perspective.

**AB:** In the same way as we can look out to the horizon and we can see it as broadly flat, but most of us have digested the idea that we live on a spherical planet, do you think that some of the things we're discovering about time right now will, in generations and centuries to come, be equally digested?

**CR:** Yeah, I think so.

**AB:** You don't think there's anything almost too counterintuitive?

**CR:** There are things that are against intuition, but intuition changes. We learn. I think we need more clarity. If we manage to survive, if we don't all kill one another in a forthcoming war, in the future some of us will be travelling and coming back younger than our peers many years later. That will obviously have a fundamental impact on our sense of time and our intuition.

**AB:** It is just so fascinating to think of the impact on humanity, the way we interact with each other, perhaps our sense of morality. What an adventure!

I've got one final thing I'd like to talk to you about. We've already touched on it a little, but it's inspiring to see how inherent to your work the arts and the humanities are. I think I said in the introduction you reference Shakespeare, Rilke, the Grateful Dead, Strauss. And this isn't just as a way to help us understand. It's not just a nice analogy for something the Grateful Dead said. This is something that runs deep for you.

**CR:** It does. And it has been particularly so with this book about time. I do think that the effort we need to bring science out of its caves will come from combining the perspectives on reality that come from science, from literature, from music and from philosophy. That's not new. The arts know that. If you read Musil, the beginning of *The Man Without Qualities,* it's all a reflection about how we make sense of what the scientists have just been telling us. To some extent this is also true for Proust. We want an integrated view of the world. We don't want a broken view of the world. The more we learn, the harder we have to work to integrate them. But that's what we need, I think.

# Jenny Zhang

## *Sour Heart*

### Tuesday 3rd July 2018

~

**Adam Biles:** *Sour Heart,* Jenny Zhang's debut short story collection, introduces readers to half a dozen girls – children, teenagers and young adults – each the daughter of Chinese immigrants to the United States, each discovering what it's like to grow up between two cultures, two languages and two histories. The stories in *Sour Heart* are raw and rich, balancing an exquisite tenderness and empathy for their protagonists with perfectly lobbed grenades of humour, often wildly scatological in tone. The book's heart may be sour, but it is also well and truly in the right place. Jenny Zhang's writing has been widely celebrated, although perhaps her most prestigious honour was one that she achieved about eight years ago, before any of her books were published, when she blew the minds of the audience in this very bookshop, winning the one and only competitive open mic night we have ever hosted. We're delighted to finally be able to welcome her back to Shakespeare and Company. Please give it up for Jenny Zhang.

**Jenny Zhang:** Thank you so much for that lovely introduction. It is the highest achievement I've ever achieved, winning an open mic here. My prize was an old pulp novel from the sixties.

**AB:** Which one was it? Do you remember?

**JZ:** I don't know, it was very trashy. I did read it. It was great!

**AB:** I'd like to begin with the title of the collection, which draws on the first story, 'We Love You Crispina'. This story sets the tone for what we're going to expect from *Sour Heart*. When you first see the title there seems something almost contradictory about the term. It's an odd turn of phrase. Could you just talk a little bit about this concept of a sour heart and what it means to the collection?

**JZ:** In the first story of this collection, 'We Love You Crispina', the nine-year-old daughter who is narrating the story, albeit retrospectively, loves sour things. She hates sweetness, she loves sourness. So instead of sweetheart, her parents call her a sour heart. As I was putting the book together, I thought that it cast the right kind of light over the entire collection because these are people who smile when it's overcast. These are people who believe that there is such a thing as 'a good kind of pain' and that there is sweetness in the sour, bitter miseries of life, and that there is something sickly about a certain kind of sweetness. So I just felt like it was a good way to encapsulate all of these narrators, who are all girls. A lot of them are greatly disliked by others, even though they really like themselves. Also, the worst thing you can be as a girl is sour. I mean, it's not actually the worst thing, but the worst thing as deemed by society is to have a sour face, a bitchy resting face, to be unlikable, to not be sweet. So I thought I would pay homage to that sentiment. Afterwards, some of my friends reminded me that sour in Chinese also means a kind of ache and it has sort of a more bitter-sweet feeling to it, which made sense.

**AB:** Your six protagonists in the book are all daughters of immigrant Chinese families. Sometimes it's dangerous to ask the author to over-explain the significance of certain things, but to me this idea of the sour heart also did seem to encapsulate the dislocation that these girls might feel living between two cultures.

**JZ:** Totally. And this feeling that you've gone bad or you've been spoiled. Not in the spoiled rotten kind of way, but like organic matter that has literally spoiled and rotted. When something sours you throw it away, it's garbage. In a figurative way these stories are about women looking back at a time in their puberty and adolescence when they were wondering 'who's going to love me and my sour heart?'

**AB:** One of the things that struck me about the collection was just how central families are. The interaction between the narrators and their families is so crucial to the way each of the stories plays out. Not only that, but we've come to expect that representations of families will be broadly negative. That's not at all what we get from your book. These are by no means perfect families, but the positivity that most of your narrators expressed towards this idea really struck me.

**JZ:** I love that you picked up on that. There is a tradition of immigrant stories, about people who are first- and second-generation people who have been displaced and dislocated. Often the story that people are used to reading, and perhaps, in America, want to hear, is the story of the second-generation kid who hates their first-generation parents, who are so crude, who are so clueless, who are so conservative, who are so ignorant, who won't let their children be free. I think it's a narrative that conveniently surfaces the idea of America being the best place on earth, and who wouldn't want to be an American, who would want to be stuck in the Old World when you could be embracing the freedom and bliss of America. I wanted to show stories where, even though these girls are mad in some ways at their families, as they get older they realise what they're angry about is the American dream, and specifically the lie of the American dream, the bullshit of the American dream, the utter abusiveness of the American dream, because it dangles something impossible in front of people who are set up to fail, and then they blame themselves and the people they come from for failing to achieve it. So I wanted to sprinkle that throughout. On the flip side, I wanted to show that, actually, these children are very attached to their families. When you've been through a battle, whether it's a physical battle, like a war, or maybe a more emotional, psychological sort of battle, you feel bonded with the people who went through it with you. These are girls who immigrate with their families during the nineties to New York City from Shanghai, and they immigrate in a very specific way and go through very similar experiences because they all come around the same time. And it's not that they want to go back to the experience of poverty and hardship and struggle, but the only people who know what that's like are their parents and their siblings and their family members and their extended community.

**AB:** One thing in all of the stories was that even though the girls were very young when they immigrated and, for the most part, fully assimilated and integrated into America, there was always this sense that home to them was with their families. There's a moment where one of the narrators says, 'this is a country that likes our food but hates our faces'. Which really demonstrates the failure of the American dream to work for these girls.

**JZ:** Right. Because the thing you're not supposed to do when you immigrate to another country is fail to assimilate. It's considered a failure. Now it's very politicised – anyone who has failed to assimilate needs to be literally deported or kicked out. This expectation that if you move to another country, you should model yourself after the dominant culture in that country. What happens if you move to another country and that country indicates daily in a nonstop, assaultive way that they hate you, that they find you repulsive, disgusting, subhuman? Why would you have any incentive to blend in when you're being told every day: 'You can't'? With the girls in these stories, if you were to speak to them on the phone, you wouldn't necessarily know what race they were. If you were to read something they wrote, you wouldn't think 'this is a Chinese person'. But when they show their faces, they're alien. So they're constantly swerving between how they feel inside and how they are regarded on the outside. When you are very in-between – whether you're an immigrant or an expat or an exile – when you're in a place where you can almost blend in, but never quite feel you have roots, where the generation before you is from elsewhere – in that way, home can be a thing that you travel with. Home can be another person. Home is not really a place, it's not a structure, it's not nationhood, but it's a relationship you have with another person. It could be a phone call you make for twenty minutes and then it's gone. It's ephemeral. On the flip side, that person can make you feel like they're not your home. There are times when these girls are talking about things they experienced at school that their parents can't relate to. Suddenly home is not with their parents. It's a constantly shifting thing.

**AB:** It concerns the expectations they grow up with as well. One of the narrators is off to Stanford. She is dealing with this idea of the life that she feels like she wants, and also the life that she feels she owes her parents to live. This seems to be a common tension in a lot of the stories, between these two sets of influences.

**JZ:** Well, it's this idea that even before you're born you're not free because someone has paid a debt for you to be born, to exist, to have food, to pursue what you want to pursue, and the enormous burden it is to feel like your life has been, and will always be, at the cost of someone else. For someone to be able to go to Stanford means that their parents can't take a vacation for twenty years. It's very hard to then feel good about doing that. At the same time, these parents are saying, 'No, please go to Stanford. We want you to go to a really good school.' But if you do that, then that means you will forever live on a plane of existence that the people who made it possible for you to exist on that plane can never arrive at or get to.

**AB:** I think, perhaps particularly for immigrants of the generation you're writing about, it's almost impossible for the children to identify with the suffering, with the hardships of their parents' generation, their grandparents' generation. And it's not like the parents try to make the children feel guilty, but the children have to process this guilt, which they take upon themselves, of not having had to live through the same experience.

**JZ:** Yeah, it's pain that's inherited but cannot necessarily be understood. It creates an obstruction of understanding on both sides. These are people who have parents who have fought in wars. The older generation is talking about a kind of pain the younger generation literally cannot even imagine. In the case of these girls, their parents are talking about things that happened in a country some of them have never even been to. On the flip side, it's hard for someone who experienced a literal tyrannical, or proto-fascist government, and famine on the scale of fifty million people dying, not to be like, 'Oh, you're being bullied at school. *That's* your problem? That's why you're crying every day? Just get over it.'

Because I'm writing from the perspective of these girls, I'm showing that it's not just that someone called me ugly, it's that every day this is the form that dehumanisation takes for me in my particular time and place, right now. But again, it's almost insulting to try and say that to someone whose friend was murdered when they were twelve.

**AB:** One of the things you do very well and very subtly in the collection is that push and pull of empathy between the generations. Certainly from the children coming to understand what their parents and grandparents experienced, but also with the way the parents almost summon the courage to empathise with the seemingly irrelevant problems of their children.

I think often when people write a collection of short stories with different narrators the temptation would be to make the narrators as distinct as possible – in part because you don't want people to think that they are all autobiographical stories, or are all broadly the same character. At the same time, the girls you're writing about, as you said earlier, in a fundamental respect do have a broadly similar experience of life. Was it a challenge for you to develop these distinct voices while also highlighting the commonality of experience between them?

**JZ:** Yeah, it was a challenge. You and I were talking before about learning how to write. If I write another book hopefully I will learn from the mistakes of this book. I look back on these stories and I see the ways in which I had failed to make them as distinct as I possibly could have. Perhaps I'll try to change that in the next book. Perhaps I will just do it again. Who knows?

I did want to show a group portrait. These are people who immigrated before Tiananmen, but after China opened up; that's actually a pretty small cohort of people. It's a very distinct cohort of people. You couldn't immigrate to America from China unless you were going as a foreign exchange student, for example. You couldn't just come from mainland China if you were a rural worker. There were very few ways for that to happen, and there were many more ways for a certain type of person to come. I do think that while, of course, women are not carbon copies of each other, because of the nature of womanhood, because of various experiences under patriarchy, a lot of women can sympathise and understand a certain experience. The same thing applies to minorities. It's not that every minority of a certain ethnicity or race or class background has the exact same tendencies and personalities. But there will be a shared commonality often. So I did want to show the ways in which they do resemble each other because they all experience such a similar and specific experience. And yet they all are quite different in very specific ways.

**AB:** I wonder if one of the elements of commonality of experience is in the interaction with the language. Language comes up as a topic in a lot of these stories because these girls are learning the language, but they're also being judged for their language abilities. From your personal experience, do you think your experimentation with language comes from living between several languages?

**JZ:** Yeah, I think so. When you're a language learner, you come off as just far more stupid than you really are. You usually have the personality of a generic nice person. It's very hard to convey your personality. I had that experience again eight years ago when I was in Paris trying to learn French. I thought: 'Oh, I really don't want to be a dumb person again.' I already was one when I was five and I was trying to learn English. I just want to get to the highest level where you can make mistakes on purpose and not by accident, where people are laughing at you because of something you intentionally said, not because of a mistake you unintentionally made. I think that because I myself immigrated from Shanghai to New York when I was five, and had that experience of becoming a baby again, where I couldn't express myself in any way, where I was, by all accounts, an idiot who was unable to form the most basic of sentences, I became very obsessed with being able to have control over language, over manipulating language. I always really loved repetition. I don't know if this is true, but when I was reading Beckett I wondered if his use of repetition came from the fact that he was always going between English and French. When you're learning a language you repeat a lot. And I love repetition. So I find myself in my writing repeating a lot. I don't know if that's because there is always the stutter of language acquisition and feeling even now there are certain words that I realise I've never heard said out loud. I've only read them in a book or I've only heard my parents say them and I'll pronounce it wrong. When I was sixteen I had never been in a car with anyone other than my parents. So when I went on this trip with my friend, who was a native white American, we were going under a tunnel and I was like, 'Oh, look, it's a *ternal*'. And they were like, 'What?' And I was like, 'ternal'. Because I'd only heard my mom and my dad say it. And that's how they said it. But what if, instead of that being humiliating to me, that was something charming and something poetic and something beautiful? So I think I tried to turn a lot of those shames into a site of creation.

**AB:** I think it shows when you come to a language in the way you did – it allows for a certain plasticity that is denied people who are born into it. You see opportunities to twist it in new ways.

Which connects to the last thing I want to talk about, which is how *Sour Heart* is an extraordinarily funny book. I don't necessarily want to use the word 'daring' because this implies there are certain things some people should say and certain things other people shouldn't. But it occurred to me that it's unusual in so-called 'immigrant literature' to find such outrageous behaviour. Is that something you have found, and do you think part of that is to do with the fact that people have been worried in the past that they might be representing a community, and therefore have to give a good impression to readers?

**JZ:** Definitely. There's this burden of responsibility when there are so few narratives; or so few voices who are allowed to be heard. If you are one of those few, then you better represent your community in a positive way, in a non-threatening way, in a non-vulgar way, a non-shameful way, in an honourable way. I think a couple of things about that. One is that there's a fetish for immigrant trauma, and to paint the wretched and the dispossessed as if they were purely good and purely virtuous and purely innocent. It's like people are worthy of our sympathy and our empathy if they are purely good people. But if they misbehave or just act human suddenly they're not worthy of it any more. So I did want to test that, test just how sour things can get. Also, when I write something that might be upsetting to people, or might be seen as shocking, I ask myself, will someone be upset because of this fictional thing I've written, or are they just upset to consider that this could happen? In this story, these two kids . . . they're kids. They're alone all the time because their parents are always working – and they grow up in a really rough and dangerous neighbourhood, and they're exposed to all kinds of stuff that they're way too young for. Kids often imitate what they see, even when they're not mentally and psychologically prepared for what that actually is. I grew up in a neighbourhood where the first time I had sex education in my elementary school, every single girl in my class at some point revealed that they had been assaulted or improperly touched by a friend or a relative or a doctor or whatever. That is disturbing. That shouldn't happen. But what's disturbing to me is the covering-up of that, the not wanting to acknowledge that because how will you change that for anyone if you don't even want to feel the discomfort of hearing it? What's not disturbing is writing about it, reading about it. So I tried to write these stories without worrying about the responsibility I had and without worrying about how people would react. But then, after I wrote them, I went back and I did consider if the harm they may cause someone was worth it – in the end, do I believe it is more important to write about it? So I did have that debate. But I tried to wait until the end of writing to have that debate with myself, because I think so often people stop themselves before they even begin. There is a fine line between exploitation and opening up a dialogue and communication. And I'm always figuring out where that line is.

I also think there's external and internal censorship, because I've heard of people of colour, including myself, saying, 'I don't want to write this because I don't want to lose the small amount of family I have. I don't want to upset people because these are things that are not talked about in my family and my community.' I feel that strongly myself. I don't necessarily know what to say about that. It can come at great cost. If you are already someone who has very tenuous family in wherever you're living, the last thing you want to do is alienate them. But also, I think, how many stories have we heard where someone was like, 'I didn't want to talk about this horrible thing that happened to me because I didn't know what my parents or my family would think'? I'm not saying that they should have talked about it, but at the very least, when you do talk about it, what does happen is all the people who felt like they should live in shame for the rest of their lives for something that happened to them, maybe they're like, 'Oh, wow, maybe I am not a disgusting cockroach on the side of the road who should shrivel up under the hot sun and die.'

# Annie Ernaux

## *The Years*

Thursday 4th October 2018

(Annie Ernaux's responses interpreted from the French by Alice Heathwood.)

~

**Adam Biles:** Spanning 1941 to 2006, *The Years* is a biography both of a woman and a nation during an era of unprecedented social flux. It's a meditation on the nature of passing time, on memories, as well as the tools and media that shape them. For Anglophone readers keen to understand contemporary France, I can't think of a better, more compelling read. Born in 1940, Annie Ernaux grew up in Normandy, studied at Rouen University and later taught at a secondary school from 1977 to 2000. Her books, in particular *A Man's Place* and *A Woman's Story* have become contemporary classics. Please join me in welcoming Annie Ernaux to Shakespeare and Company.

**Annie Ernaux:** Thank you.

**AB:** At a moment you write, 'the voices of the guests flowed together to compose the great narrative of collective events'. When composing this great narrative, a writer has to choose the grammatical pronoun. In fact you choose two: the '*nous*' (we) but also the '*elle*'(she). Why was it important to you to employ both voices?

**AE:** The choice came fairly quickly. When I started to write the book, I knew that I didn't want to use the first person. Because it's a book that I had been thinking about and which had been maturing for a long time. I knew my story couldn't be told without the surrounding history. We couldn't have the history as a sort of optional extra. At the time I wanted to start writing I was forty-five. When I looked back, I realised that my story was very much part of my generation's story. A generation that has known so many great changes and so many things happen that had never happened before. I'm really talking about for women specifically here. So I felt it was impossible to use the word 'I'. In fact, at one point I thought about only using the '*nous*' and the '*on*', the two different forms of 'we'.

**AB:** I'd like to know why you decided to write *The Years* when you did. You said the book had been maturing for a long time, and it seemed to represent a certain generation, a certain narrative arc. So what was it about 2000, when you started writing the book, that made you think that was the moment? Had something come to an end? Were we in a transitional period, into a new generation or a new world?

**AE:** The first sentences of the book – 'All the images will disappear' – and several of the other images at the start of the book, date precisely from 1995. So that was the very first idea for the book. After that I had to think a lot, and actually wrote several other books in between. As you mentioned, I was a teacher and had classes to prepare, so writing over the long term was difficult. Which was why I really started to write the book when I retired in 2000.

**AB:** Let's dwell on that first line. 'All the images will disappear.' It's a line which has an immediate impact on the reader, because it evokes the inevitable confrontation with death. There's also another moment where you talk about everything being erased in a second and vanishing into the vast anonymity of a distant generation. Was the book, in some sense, a reaction against this? Against the reality of the human condition, the desire to persist in history, when all images and all memories are finished, when all existence is finished?

**AE:** Yes. Maybe I just need to give a biographical detail which is mentioned in the book. When I wrote the lines that you just read, I did so without knowing I had breast cancer. It was detected a very short time after that. So I think there was something that was pushing me to persevere with this text. For several months, almost a year – the time in which I was being treated for the breast cancer, which had a happy outcome – I wrote a lot. I do think it was a way of fighting against time and fighting against death. That said, I've realised that in my writing time is very important. With *The Years*, even the title evokes time. I really think that time is the main character in my book.

**AB:** I think in literature we often tend to regularise time, to give everything more or less the same rhythm and representation. One of the very striking things about *The Years* is that there are moments when time expands, when time contracts, when time acts in deeply unusual ways, which we all live through but which is very rarely successfully committed to paper. Was it a challenge for you as a writer to resist the conventional ways of representing time in your writing and to represent it authentically, as you remembered it and as you had experienced it?

**AE:** No, I don't think I really had to fight against specific conventions. I instantly knew that I wanted to write time in that way. By which I mean each time I wanted to immerse myself in the particular time that I chose to write about – the 1950s, the 1960s, 1968 – I really wanted to rediscover the taste and the colour of that time, of those years. With lots of personal memories, of course, photos, but also collective memories. So political events, events in the news and songs. Every time it really is a break with the present. I wanted to immerse the reader in the details of that time. It was the only way for me to find that time again. I didn't wonder if there was another way I could write about it.

**AB:** When you are recalling these moments – when you are remembering the forties, the fifties, the sixties – throughout the book, you use photos, films and videos as aides-memoir. I'd like to hear your thoughts about how these objects affect the memories themselves and how they act as a means to access these memories. Did you have a sense that the presence of those photos and other media throughout your life had changed the memories themselves?

**AE:** I'm going to give you a very clear response to this question: the photos have absolutely no relation to my memory. The photos are there to introduce a generalist and collective narrative: a person, a girl, who becomes a woman. At the start I had no plan at all to put photos in the book. I realised I was writing something that was becoming too impersonal, too cold. So the photos seemed to introduce her presence in the book. They also became a way to anchor the story in an epoch. The way the little girl is dressed also represents their social and economic background. They transmit a lot of meaning. In addition – and here you are right – I have attached memories to the photos. As beings with memory, you live in the present and you have your past, but you also look to the future. So it was a lot of effort to go back to the photos and consider not only the present of the girl who was twelve, or the girl who was sixteen, but also how she saw the future that was to come.

**AB:** This question of how we see the future to come and – particularly in the period covered by *The Years* – how girls and women saw the future, is crucial to the book. It also presents a certain paradox. There are plenty of advances, and there are inventions like the contraceptive pill. And yet at the same time, later on in the book you write, 'We no longer knew if the women's revolution really happened.' Looking back, and particularly with the context we're living in – with a very vocal and very present women's movement, the MeToo movement – what is your opinion about the women's revolution now? Are you more convinced it has happened or not?

**AE:** I finished my book at the end of 2007, and at that time I really thought that the women's revolution had not taken place, that there had even been a sort of backwards movement towards a very traditional vision of women. I mean, 'feminist' had become a taboo word. We say that jokingly now, but it was true. I think maybe that's been changing for the last ten years. MeToo seemed to come out of nowhere, but that's not true. I think the generation of women who were, let's say, twenty years old in 2010, really had a different attitude to virility and to male privilege. So things have changed. But when it all happened about a year ago, I think it was a really wonderful, happy surprise for me. I remember writing a few months, or maybe a year, beforehand in my diary that I think I will die without having seen the women's revolution. Now, while it's not finished yet, I think important steps have been taken.

**AB:** I guess that whenever there is a social advance, there's always the fear that there will be a retreat, or that the results won't be what one hopes, or what one expects. In *The Years* the events of May 1968 are a pivotal moment for society and for the collective voice in the book. But quite quickly afterwards we see, not exactly the rejection of many of the declarations that were made at that time, but perhaps their absorption into this view of consumerism, the capitalist worldview. Do you consider May 1968, despite it occupying a pivotal role in the book, something of a disappointment?

**AE:** I think you have to understand that in the years following '68 there was in fact a sort of liberation, an optimism, a lack of fear of the future. Now I think things are basically the opposite. It really was something that was felt across all different levels of society. Now, little by little, it's closed off. There was a sort of resurgence in '81 with the election of François Mitterrand, but very quickly the eighties became really sad years with the rise of triumphant liberalism. But that was a global phenomenon. It's true that consumerism came along at the same time as '68, and there was a kind of conversion from desiring ideals to desiring consumer goods. There was an appetite for *things*. But you have to realise that in my book I don't condemn it. It wasn't written as a judgement of history. It's really written to show how history passes through us, how it passed through me. Of course, you can glimpse little political preferences, but I really didn't write it to judge.

# Rachel Cusk

## *Kudos*

### Thursday 29th November 2018

~

**Adam Biles:** Faye is on a plane again. We met her first in *Outline*, teaching a creative writing course in Athens, then in *Transit*, constructing a new life for her family in London. In *Kudos*, she's on the move once more, travelling from one author engagement to another. We come to know Faye through a succession of conversations, almost monologues, during which she withholds and her interlocutor holds forth. These conversations are many and varied, and yet are repeatedly drawn towards certain themes – womanhood, motherhood, marriage and divorce; the writer's life, her role, and the expectations placed upon her by readers, audiences and journalists – as well as the points where all these subjects intersect and overlap. Please join me in welcoming Rachel Cusk to Shakespeare and Company.

**Rachel Cusk:** Thank you.

**AB:** We're here tonight to talk about *Kudos*, but it's difficult to do so without also talking about *Outline* and *Transit*. It's very rare, I think, to come across even one book that is able to sustain a harmony of form, of tone, of content across its length, and you've managed to do it over three. So I'm intrigued by the genesis of your approach. Did you have a subject, and the form and tone developed from this subject? Or did the technical restraints come first, and then you found what to fill them with afterwards?

**RC:** It would have been nice if it had just developed in that lovely way you described. Actually it was like breaking rocks by the side of the road. It was very hard to work it out. And it came out of the feeling that the forms in which I had written before were sort of binary. I'd written novels, but there was some material that, for some reason, I couldn't put in. The novel wasn't the right form. So for a while I wrote in the memoir form, because that seemed to me the best available form for what I wanted to say. But it became completely obvious to me that, particularly, the memoir form malfunctioned, and that offering oneself as an example, which is how I used it – and that was to talk about aspects of life where there had to *be* an example – expecting somebody to make the transition into fictional representation wasn't right. Motherhood was a very good example of that. You had to say 'I'. And I didn't care. I was just offering the 'I'. But the malfunction, I would say, created the opportunity for people to seize the 'I' and use it to distance the material from themselves. So it didn't work, and I ended up being very violently criticised for those books. So that gave me pause. I thought: 'OK, how can you speak without presenting yourself as a target?' I think that is specifically to do with being female. I think that, you know, a Knausgaard does the same thing but because he's male, white, Scandinavian, the target is of no particular interest. No one needs to defend themselves against that honesty.

**AB:** People have talked about the form you landed on for these novels as a reinvention of the novel, but it seems from what you're saying that this new form didn't necessarily come out of the desire to do something new, but almost out of a need.

**RC:** Anyone in a crisis of living, of identity, has to consider whether they're going to doggedly carry on or whether they're going to change. Change is frightening. But it's essential. I suppose I didn't realise how much of what I saw as change was also a change of the form itself, and that it was an opportunity to break some new ground.

**AB:** Once you had landed on the form, the means of expressing what you wanted to express, and achieving it with *Outline*, was there then a sort of *post facto* establishing of rules for the next book?

**RC:** There was an establishing of rules right from the start. The issue of self-control is a really interesting one when you're trying to say things that still have some radicalness – if that's a word – about them. For me it remains radical to talk about femininity and female experience. I think when you're documenting new bits of life, the issue of self-control and discipline seems slightly remote, and that seems like something that belongs to an academic view of life that I'd rather neglected – or at least I went elsewhere to seek those things, to educate myself, to know. But I don't think I had asked great self-control of myself. I had asked precision and bravery and lots of other things, but not that. So this really required me to not go into a particular space. And writing it, from the first sentence of *Outline* to the last sentence of *Kudos,* was the same feeling. I would start to drive down a sentence and have to reverse out of it because it was a sentence that was like the sentence equivalent of Fifth Avenue. It was a sentence that everyone went down and where all the bad things could happen. I had to not do that.

**AB:** Was there not, then, the concurrent sense of liberation within the constraints, such as schools like the Oulipo talk about? Where by adding mathematical restraints they get a sense of freedom?

**RC:** Absolutely. It's like poetry: it's hard to write a sonnet, but it's easier to write a sonnet, because it has rules, than to write free verse. Once I understood it, it was completely technical. What I had understood about what was going wrong in this form – and not just in my own work, in other people's work too – was totally technical. And that wasn't a criticism. It was a sort of dawning realisation that I happened to have. But the unfortunate result is it's made it really hard for me to read.

**AB:** There was a sensation I had when reading these books that they could not have been written by a man. There was something so deeply connected to the fact that the protagonist was a woman – the fact that you're a woman. There was something that would have prohibited a man from taking this approach.

**RC:** I think it's much more about being in the margins. I'd say probably the biggest key I got was from Camus. Camus's persona, the person watching in a lot of what he writes, is a marginal person. I agree that in this project, the femininity of the narrator is necessary because the very first thing that had to be disposed of was the author trying to convince the reader that they have not written the book. You know, the author makes their narrator a neuroscientist, and has to spend 500 pages showing how much they know about neuroscience. I didn't want to waste anybody's energy on that game.

**AB:** I try not to read around the books I'm going to talk about because I think that can inform too much the questions I'm going to ask. But I did see in a couple of press quotes people referring to these books as autofiction. I thought that was interesting, just because the narrator is very clearly named Faye. This is a sort of a signifier that – whether there are elements of it that are similar to your life or not – a line is being drawn.

**RC:** I'm essentially a conservative in the sense that I feel I exist in reference to a classical tradition. The writer of autofiction is in a sense better aligned to modernity. But I feel that we are all people who arrived at a roadblock. I went this way, and they went that way, but essentially we're just trying to get around the same thing. And to me, what a Sheila Heti or a Knausgaard is doing is utterly different from what I'm doing. But it's a response to the same thing.

**AB:** So this label of autofiction that has been put on these books by certain people, is that something that you would reject?

**RC:** I don't recognise that in how I made these books. It might be how they look. But it's not how I made them.

**AB:** You spoke earlier about not wanting to expose yourself in the novels, not wanting to leave yourself open to people pinning certain things on you. This absence of Faye from the novels could be seen as a sense of retreat. And yet, while reading *Kudos*, it dawned on me that there's a strength to it as well.

**RC:** I think it's also just how existence is configured. I had entered such dangerous waters with the memoirs I had written. I don't know how strong other writers are in terms of dealing with criticism, but it was an extraordinary attack that I was subjected to. So I guess there was a reason to think about this question of self. Does the truth-teller have to be a kind of Jesus-person? The person who comes out and says, 'OK, you can do what you want to me, but I'm going to sacrifice myself, I'm putting myself in front of you for you to do your worst.' Then I thought: 'Well, actually, there's a moral problem with the novel rather than with the people who read and write them. There's a problem with this form that says that you can deeply inhabit another person.' Yet it's why you read books, because the feeling of inhabiting another consciousness can be so consoling. And that should still be OK. I was talking to somebody yesterday about the Brontë sisters and the experience of going to the Brontë parsonage. The three Brontës created, for someone like me, the whole concept of living in a book. Removing you from your own existence, from the experience of being yourself. Then you go into the little museum by the parsonage, and it tells you that in the time they lived in this village, on top of this hill, there was extraordinary child mortality because they had an open sewer and the community hadn't worked out that it was running into the water supply. Is that ever mentioned in any of their books? No, it isn't. And so, what is the relationship between these two things? Between reality and this thing, this world that you can go and live in? I guess I think the novel has become so far removed even from that, in terms of this idea that you can inhabit another consciousness, that if the writer is inhabiting another consciousness and then inhabiting their habitation of that, this seemed to me where the problem lay.

**AB:** It seems also to presuppose that there is a consistent consciousness to inhabit. As if there's just one for each of us, one comprehensible consciousness, rather than something which is fluid, and which is changing all the time.

**RC:** And that it can choose not to remember anything, can choose not to be itself tomorrow if it doesn't want to be. How much of this version of identity that we're given in books, how much does it actually construct us, construct what we think our lives ought to be? Why do we choose to remember anything or identify with anything? Once you start to unpick that — really almost coldheartedly and not as a human, just as a technician, which is what I was doing — and see what it does to sentences and see how this subjectivity is created, it almost is sickening. You almost can't bear it any more.

**AB:** That seems to apply to the subject of the family as well. How does one talk in any sort of authentic way about what being in a family is. One of the things that makes this book so strong on the subject of the family is that we get this multiplicity of voices and family experiences. We're being given lots of different approaches to the family, and also a sense that none of the people who are talking really seem to be able to understand the dynamic of the family that they're coming from.

**RC:** You know, any chink that you leave open to judgement, people will judge you. The particular chink in these books is the fact that all three of them occur in a fairly short space of time, four or five days, when the narrator is not with her children. That is the occasion of the novels. That's why she is writing this novel. She's able to think in this way because she's not at home in the kitchen being how she usually is. So I suppose that slightly creates a premise of a particular kind of abandoning, or dysfunctional world of the family. But I really hope that people haven't taken it as that. I don't read reviews very much, but I'm pretty sure that one of the things that's said is that everybody sounds like the narrator, or they all sound the same, essentially, and that this is really strange. Why do these people all sound the same? I guess that was my attempt to break down the feeling of reality — or a false feeling of reality — that people have about their own struc-tured lives, in which there are judgements such as whether you spend enough time with your children. I wanted to achieve some-thing much more oceanic in terms of how we're the product of our moment in history, of the place where we live. It's like you're drinking the water in a place and it's part of you, but you're also you. And I think that's so true of these themes of family life. We can seem so alien to one another, but I suppose I've just tried to find a line, which is talking, where everyone brings themselves to a moral location.

**AB:** On the subject of talking. When reading the books, you get a sense that these people seem disposed to hold forth to Faye and divulge things about their lives. In that way it's reminiscent of the confessional or a psychoanalytical session. I wonder if that feeds into what you were just saying about that sense of bringing people together through these multiple conversations. I don't want to say it's like a form of group therapy, but . . .

**RC:** Oh no, it is! It's completely based on that. Or not completely, but the therapeutic model is definitely part of it. And when you see and indeed think about your own life in these terms, it becomes clear that there are moments in which you've lived in a state of great belief about your own life and other times when you can look at it dispassionately, objectively. I saw this family on the train coming over here, and it's clear they can barely notice what other people's reality is. Because for them, you know, the drama of being them is completely compelling and that's what they're doing. I wanted to get people in a state where they're more anonymous – out on the street, as it were, alone among others. They're not in this drama. They can see themselves in each other slightly more clearly. Some of the style of the book is my true belief that people have a very natural grasp of form, in talking and recounting stories. It's something that we learn to do the second we can talk. How was school today? You know, the kid tells the story of it. And if people laugh at a particular point, the next day he'll enlarge that bit. Everybody does it. And the idea that that is something that could almost be called writing was, I suppose, kind of the foundation.

**AB:** A sort of structuring of understandable narrative for the chaos of our own lives, almost.

**RC:** Yes. And that is the therapeutic model, which in itself is also a kind of writing.

**AB:** It's interesting to think of that, because I was trying to understand when rereading the books if there was a sense immediately that they were destined to be a trilogy. When reading *Outline* there's definitely a sense that you're prepping the reader for what's to come in very subtle ways. It's only once you know what's coming after that you have a sense of what groundwork was being laid. Conversely in *Kudos* I felt there was a sense of reflection on what had come before.

**RC:** At that point I thought, 'I've been doing this for six years or something, and I can kind of make a few jokes about it', which I did.

**AB:** But was the trilogy structure locked in for you from the beginning?

**RC:** No, only in as much as I always end things as soon as I possibly can. I'm the person who's clearing the plates away from the table before everyone's quite finished eating dinner. I've never written a really long book. I don't think I have the confidence, or the feeling of entitlement or relaxation to do that. For me, the writing of a book is such a high-wire act. It's amazing to be on it, but then I really need to get off it, or to know when I'm going to get off it. So I think the trilogy was the only way I could write at a much bigger scale. Essentially it is one long book, but I had to do it in these parts. I understood at the end of *Outline* that I had asked more questions than I'd answered. And that actually it was all very well to have this – not nihilistic, exactly, but unbodied – narrator, but at a certain point, she has to go back to her life and live in a house and live in a body and relate to people. I mean, she could just swim off into the sea, which she considers doing at a certain point. But she doesn't, as people generally don't. So it was a question of acknowledging that actually some of the causes of the project, which were also the causes of my anger, had to be addressed. And it has taken fully three books to get there.

**AB:** I suppose writing and publishing them two years apart, particularly with *Kudos*, allowed outside events to intervene. So, perhaps inevitably in a British novel written between 2014 and 2018, Brexit makes a few appearances. But this also allows a reflection on this idea of withholding opinions and feelings. You write, 'I said it was true that the question of whether to leave or remain was one we usually ask ourselves in private, the final surrender of personal consciousness into the public domain.' It suddenly made me think that we do perhaps live in an age in which the pressure is to get everything out there, everything one's feeling, to define oneself. And the fact that Faye doesn't do that in these books is some sort of political act in itself.

**RC:** There are two questions there. Brexit in a lot of ways is sort of tailor-made for me, because it's a divorce. It's a public example of the private theme that I've been interested in the last few years. I'm very wary of allowing current events and politics to make their mark in a piece of work. It seems ridiculous to quote Hemingway in this bookshop but I'm going to do it. I think he said: 'You can put in the politics if you like, but in ten years' time, those are the pages that everyone's just going to be turning over and not reading.' And I kind of agree with that. I guess instead you have to make those politics into a structure. And to me, that was what I was trying to do. I just took a gamble and thought: 'These are the same themes, and they are suddenly cropping up at the very surface of our society rather than just in specific stories about people's lives.'

**AB:** And about withholding being a kind of a political act in an age where people are encouraged to express?

**RC:** I think that's something that I didn't think of as meaning anything beyond my own self when I began *Outline*. Now I think actually the value of silence is becoming clearer and clearer. And it's so interesting, to any writer, it's interesting and frightening to be made aware of the culpability of language, the dangerous possibilities of language, to have to develop a new consciousness of the fact that we might have to use language more morally and be more careful in what we say. And then who gets to say anything is the other thing. Despite the fact that I did arrive at these realisations, it still seemed a morally unobjectionable idea to simply read the surface. But I also continue to feel unsure of what I'm allowed to say, of whether I will continue to be allowed to say anything, which is kind of strange.

**AB:** I want to finish with the subject of literary events. It's almost impossible not to when a book, or particularly *Outline* and *Kudos*, involve so many . . .

**RC:** It's a funny one, isn't it? I'm in dangerous waters with this one.

**AB:** Yeah! But talking about the world of books generally. There are a couple of very striking pages in *Kudos* talking about the state of literature now, and of publishing. There's a moment when a publisher is speaking and they say, 'we publishers proceed on the assumption that no one cares about books' or that 'we're always being threatened with extinction, as though novels likewise had once been fierce and were now fragile and defenceless.' So my final question tonight is about the potential role of the novel. Do you see the world as one in which novels can still make an impact in the way perhaps they did in previous generations?

**RC:** It depends who's writing them and how they're being written. I think that the whole idea of literature or of any art being sacred is very much to blame. Why should the novel be supported, be helped to exist if there has been an outliving of its usefulness? It's this idea that reading is sacred, that it's good for children, that reading is morally beneficial rather than just being a form of escapism. People can do what they want. If this bookshop chooses to start selling hamburgers instead of books, that is not a moral crime. What I see is maybe a certain kind of literature possibly becoming extinct out of surfeit – as maybe we're all going to become extinct – just by there being too much of it, an over-supply. And then other kinds of literature which have this wonderful role to play in fortifying individuals, which is what it's about. Ignoring the group, refusing to try to please the group, saying the individual is what matters. That is what a book does. It is one individual talking to another individual and that is its strength. And I still see it. I see it as alive as ever, just not where anybody thinks it is. But I see it as alive as ever. Just not winning prizes.

# Meena Kandasamy

## *When I Hit You*

### Tuesday 5th March 2019

~

**Adam Biles:** Every so often the novel is called into question. What relevance does this bourgeois, centuries-old literary form have to modern life? Surely the time when a work of literature can shock us, unsettle us, genuinely get under our skin and make us apprehend the world in a fundamentally different way is long past? *When I Hit You* is a one-book rebuttal of such claims. When we meet our narrator, we learn that she has escaped, survived, an abusive marriage. The central question of the book is established at once as not *if* she gets out, but *how*. *When I Hit You* is a searing indictment of the structures, physical, emotional, societal and linguistic, that conspire to imprison women in violent relationships. It exposes the complicity each of us bears in sustaining these structures, consciously or unconsciously, through what we pretend not to hear and choose not to see. But Meena Kandasamy's novel is also, crucially, a courageous demonstration of how one woman dismantles these cages. In this way, *When I Hit You* is not just the account of an escape, but a tool for empowerment. Please welcome Meena Kandasamy.

**Meena Kandasamy:** Thanks for that beautiful introduction.

**AB:** I want to begin not so much at the beginning of the book, but at the beginning of the relationship that is central to this book. What we see very quickly when we meet our narrator's husband is his ability to build up structures of control in the relationship. Now some of these are physical structures – he moves them to a town in which she has no connections. Others are technological or social – he cuts her off from her friends, from her social networks, from internet access. So my first question is, given our narrator is an incredibly intelligent, forceful, opinionated woman, how is it that these structures grow around her?

**MK:** This, I may say, is a challenging question. I think when we start talking about why this book was written, part of it is because when I set out to write I was aware that writing about Indian women in an abusive, violent marriage is a cliché. I think in the same way, as an Indian myself, growing up I would have thought, 'Oh, another book on marriage.' And then this kind of thing happens to you and you step back. So something I encounter all the time – both from my own experience, and from the experience of a lot of other people – is the question about how it happens to fierce women. Because you're fierce and you're a woman, you're not allowed to have this happen to you. These are the expectations that are put on women.

But I think at the heart of it, is that when women are strong – and I have personally felt this not only within marriage, but in a lot of circumstances – it gives men a lot of extra brownie points for bringing you down, for intimidating you, for hurting you. The stronger you come across, the more it becomes a challenge to actually exert patriarchal control. But going beyond any individual, violence is often a creation of social conditions. We come from a society where there are people who are considered untouchable, there is the caste system: in which you're high in the hierarchy, or low in the hierarchy. But all of this control is how society replicates itself, isn't it? Women are supposed to marry within their caste, or entire villages are going to be burned. The threat of violence is what keeps all of these structures in place. When you come from a society where there's so much violence invested in keeping structures in place, you can easily see why this would be applied to small things like the family unit. It can be applied from husband to wife. It can be applied from parents to children. I think that's also why this has to be a broader conversation on violence and gender, social structures and gender.

**AB:** One thing that really surprised me – and I suppose this is connected to the clichés you talked about earlier – is how there are some things about their relationship which seem very specific to Indian society, and others which apply to relationships the world over. For instance, I don't think someone who has spent their entire life in Europe or the United States would feel themselves confronted with an entirely unfamiliar situation.

**MK:** One of the things of labelling somebody as Indian, or talking about the typical Indian novel or seeing something as representative, is that it very rarely is. Not all Indian girls are getting married to Maoist guerrillas. But I think women around the world are facing similar oppressions, and not necessarily within marriage. Even in relationships that are not necessarily violent. I'm not blaming them for it, but a lot of people have reduced the book to being about physical violence. But for me the idea was also how very humiliating it is for a woman when you're not recognised for who you are, or your intellect is not recognised. For me, I think part of writing in this way was also to ask – and this is a conversation that's happening in the Left as we speak – about what place women have in the revolution and how feminism is always being pushed to the margins. So for me, it's a very political question. I think that's why women outside of India relate to it, because they have been told to shut up, they're privileged. They've been called out for complaining.

**AB:** The husband, as you said, was a Maoist guerrilla. He's a political science lecturer at a college and, in a sense, uses Communist ideology as a weapon to oppress his wife. It did get me thinking, more broadly, about whether there is an inherent violence to ideologies generally.

**MK:** No. I wouldn't say that. I think on the question of violence, I would have a very different opinion. I can't be governed by a pacifist who says all violence is bad. Because the violence of an oppressed people is different from the violence used to oppress people. So I don't think I would completely reject ideology. What I would say is that when we don't call out male misogyny for what it is, when we don't call out male entitlement for what it is, then any ideology can be twisted to become a tool of patriarchy. Even a revolutionary ideology which fights for everybody's equality and social justice, or whatever the Left broadly stands for, can become another space for men to just put in their own claim. That's why it becomes a feminist concern to actually challenge what's happening, because the men who quote the Bible or Hindu religious texts to say, 'Oh, this is the place of women' also have no problem in quoting *The Communist Manifesto.* So the problem here is inherent sexism which has to be called out.

**AB:** There's a moment where you write that she fell in love with him because when he spoke about the Revolution, it seemed more intense than any poetry. This is perhaps a naive thing to say, but the ideology of the Left being used in this pernicious way surprised me, I think because of inherited beliefs I have about the Left's adherence to justice and to social progress.

**MK:** Absolutely. It's an interesting question because, for instance, in the UK everybody is talking right now about Shamima Begum's radicalisation. But when people talk about radicalisation, and how young people are easily 'radicalised', what they are really talking about is how these people want to change the world around them. I think we have to accept that as the beginning point – not 'oh, they're running off to join the terrorists'. There's a big demarcation between the two. Young people are saying, enough is enough. So that's why I think I would still find a demonstration more beautiful than poetry.

**AB:** Do you think the violence of the relationship was allowed to grow and install itself almost because we refuse to accept for a while that somebody with these professed beliefs could be acting in a way that seems so contradictory?

**MK:** Do I think women are to blame for the violence that happens to them? No. Do I think women are to be blamed for allowing it to fester? No. That's also why this book is called autofiction. A lot of people call it a memoir and I'm like, 'No, please allow women at least the freedom to define what we write.' If I had called it a memoir and said, 'this is my life story', there would have been so much passivity to that. It's like all these things *happened* to me. You spoke about the novel being a bourgeois form, but I think it's actually a very Western idea to think of literature as a leisure activity. For some of us, it's life. So when I was writing, I was not only creating this work, but I was creating myself. When we think of fiction it's often as a book on the shelf. But fiction is also if a woman tells her abusive husband, 'I will never leave you' when she's basically buying time. This fiction is something she's imagining. It is an act of creativity. I think all of us are creating these fictions which make life easier. In that sense, I don't think fiction has to be removed and seen as some kind of fraud. Fiction and narratives exist because they are part of who we are and how we present ourselves. How I present myself to you, to people here, to my partner at home. This process is very active. If I was living in France, in the UK, I would have just called the police and that would be the end of my story. But in Indian society it's entirely different. People would be like, 'She possibly met somebody at the reading, you know? And that's why she decided to leave her husband.' People would not believe that somebody was being violent and abusive. So you have to stay long enough to let people know this was happening, or try other avenues. You are creating this narrative because you have to tell a story that people find credible. It's not only novels that are plot-driven. People expect lives to be plot-driven too.

**AB:** One thing that is central to *When I Hit You* is the role that language plays as a tool of violence. And yet our narrator discovers at a certain moment that language can be the source of liberation as well.

**MK:** I think I obsess about this language question a lot because I write in my second language, which is English. I think language actually allows you to become a different person.

**AB:** In one sense, language is what you have control over, but in another sense you don't have control over it, because if the situations in which you're obliged to operate limit your vocabulary, that can limit the way you reflect about the world. That's something you feel while reading this book. That the narrator doesn't feel as if there are options, as if each potential exit is closed almost immediately because of the different ways people react through language. For example, you talk about something you call the 'politeness phenomenon', in which the structures of these polite formulations don't allow us to talk about these situations of violence.

**MK:** I'll answer this, not by going into the novel, but as somebody who started living in London. I met my partner five years ago, and we were always going back and forth between India and here. He was the only one with a job, so it became my chance to move. Anyway, in London people would say 'How are you?' and I would start explaining my day to them, or tell them what was wrong or something my mum had said. And then after a long time, I realised that you're just supposed to say 'alright', 'fine'. I'm not supposed to actually share my whole history. I'm just supposed to say 'How are you?' back. That's the politeness phenomenon. So, yeah. That's just a commentary. It's nothing to do with the book really.

**AB:** But I think it is connected to the book because it shows that even formulations like that, which are very well meant, or meant in a neutral fashion, still have a capacity to oppress.

**MK:** Yeah, like a lot of the questions that are directed at women contain huge pressure. You're expected to bear children by a certain age, and all these Indian aunties are like, 'Oh, do you have any good news?' Which means, are you expecting? Or, 'When is your wedding?' This is not just social control, but a huge heteronormativity. I'm sure it's a problem in every culture, but I can only speak for my own. The question about marriage being forced onto young people also drives a lot of young people into relationships they wouldn't otherwise be in. 'When are you getting married?', 'When are you going to have your baby?'. It's very intrusive.

**AB:** And indeed, we see that with the family in the book. The mother and father are very sympathetic characters when we meet them. And yet they seem unable to engage with what she is telling them about the relationship, and respond in what feels like quite a formulaic way, perhaps dictated by the society.

**MK:** Yeah. And that's when you realise how powerful performance is. You'd rather have your daughter in the bad relationship than have society throwing mud at you. There's a lot of social regimentation, especially in the caste society. People are absolutely paranoid about what their local caste is going to say.

I'm very interested in archival material, and have looked at a lot of British legislation and colonial documents. The one big question is: does the caste have the right to expel its members? Does the member have the right to appeal? If a caste decides that somebody should do something and this person doesn't do it, they can be expelled. I think when we talk about India, this is the kind of absolute structure within which all of this operates. So when people wonder what will the neighbours say, it's the fear of ridicule and of being excluded or ostracised.

**AB:** The narrator is not immune to these feelings herself. She wonders what people would think. And she worries about how ridiculous she would look leaving a marriage after one or two months.

**MK:** We all internalise that reality.

**AB:** Which makes her question herself.

**MK:** Absolutely. Because, as I said earlier, one of the things about any kind of decision-making is not how you rationalise it to yourself, but how you rationalise it to others. We exist within society. So as much as we reject its oppressions, we have to respond to them or at least be aware of what we are rebelling against and what we are stepping outside of.

**AB:** There does seem to be a tipping point, which is the moment the husband uses the most extreme form of control: he rapes her. That seems to be the tipping point for her parents as well. That's a moment where a line has been crossed and they can no longer accept that.

**MK:** Yeah, that's a question which is quite interesting. At the moment we are living through the MeToo movement and women are speaking out. But in Hindi cinema, rape almost becomes a spectacle. So the idea of rape installed in the public imagination is something like that. And I think this kind of extreme structuring of the woman's lack of consent makes people not actually respond to it, or every instance of it, because it happens all the time. One of the things when I was writing was dealing with the fact that I was coming from a culture where rape is a word that you don't utter, where nobody speaks about it, or calls it by its right name. Rape is something that happens to a Bandit Queen or something. It's a gory spectacle where men blindfold you and there's all this horrible music in the background, and then the woman is shown with blood and cuts on her face. I'm not denying this happens as well. But in pretending that rape only happens in the most extreme circumstances, we take away from its everyday-ness. But this everyday-ness is a reality to a lot of people. Which means that women's consent always gets glossed over, or erased, or trivialised.

And don't forget that in India marital rape is not even criminalised. Law reflects what men are thinking. So you have to draw that out. And at the same time, you have to write about these things without it becoming trauma porn. Because you don't want to sit here and play the victim. In writing this book it was very important to me that it be intellectual. When you happen to be a woman of colour, what inevitably happens is that you get asked to write about horrible things that have happened to you, or about horrible things happening in the place where you come from. But with this book, and with most of what I'm trying to write, I want to go over that and talk about situations which could equally happen in the UK. Because it's not very different in terms of the violence against women. It may not be on the same scale, but the misogyny still exists. And I had to draw that out.

**AB:** One of the ways you draw it out is through the defiant humour present in the book. There are moments that are almost absurdist. Is that part of a survival mechanism? Does the recognition that the husband is ultimately ridiculous provide a source of strength in a way?

**MK:** Oh, I think it's definitely a survival mechanism. Recently something happened which had never happened to me before, and I was so surprised to learn that about myself. I was in a meeting and a very elderly white British woman was complaining about the time she spent in Brazil, and she said, 'There's no public transport. The rich could just take a plane and fly, but the poor people had to go by bus for three days.' Then, she said, 'See, at least in India, the British gave the railways.' I heard that and I just started laughing, and I couldn't stop. After all these years, after all of this, that's what you go to? Colonialism is bad, but sometimes you have to laugh at it. In the same way misogyny is bad, but sometimes it can be so carelessly stupid that it elicits a kind of laughter mechanism.

**AB:** It makes me think of that very famous piece of film from just before Ceauşescu was deposed. He's giving a speech, with his wife next to him, and hasn't been challenged for four decades. And suddenly someone in the crowd starts heckling him. And then others start laughing at what he's saying. And he was gone within a few days. That came to me when reading this book because you realise that there is an absolute power in that.

**MK:** It's ridiculous. Laughing at somebody is actually a challenge to authority without being a verbal challenge to authority.

**AB:** In recognising that ridiculous side, and in recognising the mechanical side to his power, she starts to take back control when she realises that she can press her husband's buttons. She knows exactly what to say to set him off into one of his rages, or to stop him going into a rage. She realises that actually that is a certain power that she has over him. And through that she starts to sow the seeds of her escape.

**MK:** I think I'm just now realising that children get this kind of thing very early on. What buttons to push so that parents yield completely to what they want them to do. But I also think that, as writers, we are constantly making these observations about other people: 'This is what that person wants and this is what this person is after.' Which is a very cynical thing to do. It's not how trust is built. But if you step out, then you can play and you can push these buttons. In some circumstances, it can be the right thing to do, but it can also be used for very manipulative reasons.

**AB:** But I guess that's the crucial point. It brings us back to that idea of writing and the narrative as a form of liberation. I'm thinking of two particular things you wrote. You say the number one lesson you've learned as a writer is to not let people remove you from your own story. The second is you say you remind yourself of the fundamental notion of what it means to be a writer: a writer is one who controls the narrative. Those two things combined seem to be the seeds of her way out of all this.

**MK:** The first book that I worked on was writing for a social cause, about the Kilvenmani massacre. In 1968, forty-four people were killed because they were striking for higher wages. They were living under extremely feudal conditions. For me, it was important to reclaim this narrative. Because the most oppressed are always written out of history, even when they pay with their lives. As I was going to fictionalise it in the form of a novel, I was also very much questioning the idea of who I was to write it. I'm somebody who lives in the city. I'm somebody who writes in English, for heaven's sake! Why am I writing a novel about this? But then the thought is, 'but you have to write this into history'. And I think it's the same logic that operates here. This woman's being abused, but she has to reclaim her narrative. Once you understand the historicity of it, it's no longer trivial to be thinking of it as one person's story. It's what's happening to women all the time. I think that's why, you know, in a sense, this kind of book could have come out anywhere.

# Madeline Miller

## *Circe*

Tuesday 2nd April 2019

~

**Adam Biles:** Few tales have been told and told again more than the Greek myths. What has slowly been acknowledged over recent generations is the significance of who does the telling. Often, as Madeline Miller has Circe observe at one moment, 'humbling women seems to me a chief pastime of poets. As if there can be no story unless we crawl and weep.' The daughter of Helios and Perse, Circe is scorned for her ungodlike appearance. When an act of sorcery sees her banished, she is forced to defend herself against the many threats that the world, ancient and modern alike, lines up for solitary women. The fact that Circe's complex character is far from given the space it deserves in Homer makes her a perfect candidate for a repositioning at the centre of the story. One of the many extraordinary things about *Circe* is how Miller can tack close to the established myths, while also making readers feel they're experiencing these stories as if for the very first time. She achieves this through her lyrical but modern prose, and her compassionate psychological engagement with her characters. Please join me in welcoming Madeline Miller to Shakespeare and Company.

One thing that sets *Circe* apart from most encounters we have with the Greek myths is the use of the first person. Immediately on the first page we have her voice. What motivated that decision?

**MM:** In your lovely introduction you mentioned my interest in the psychology of the characters. Homer in *The Iliad* and *The Odyssey* does not really give psychology. He implies it, but he's not really connecting the psychological dots. He's never giving you Hamlet's soliloquy. That's just not the epic style. So part of what I wanted was to do a deep dive into the psychology of this character. But it also felt really important to use the 'I' because Circe's story in *The Odyssey* is actually narrated by Odysseus. When you start looking at the episode from that perspective, you start realising how incredibly self-serving it is. Here's Odysseus saying, 'I came to this island, there's a terrifying witch, but I tamed her. And then she threw herself at me'. He goes on and on about how beautiful she is. And every time he says that, what he's really saying is, 'look how important I am. This goddess wants to be with me.' So part of what I wanted to do was strip away Odysseus, his self-aggrandising. I felt like it was doubly biased. First of all, it was the heroic male, traditional, epic narrative. Then you have Odysseus, the great liar of ancient literature layered on top of it.

**AB:** And once you decided upon that, did Circe's voice come to you quite quickly?

**MM:** Not at all. It took me five years. I think part of that was that I had lived with Patroclus in my mind for ten years. I had to write Patroclus out and say goodbye to him and find Circe. And I wanted her voice to be very different. For me, finding a character's voice is trial and error. I write and I throw away and I write again. Now that I have written the novel, I can articulate what I wanted for her voice. But at the time, it's just me wandering in the woods, trying stuff out. And actually, around year five, I said, 'I guess I can't do it. I can't do it.' I took a break, which is what I always do when I get stuck. I started working on a novel inspired by *The Tempest*, which is also about witches and magic and islands. And somehow that untangled whatever I needed to untangle. When I came back to the *Circe* manuscript, which was by then a thousand pages of junk, I was able to pick the three things out that were right and put them together. So once I do have the voice it comes very quickly for me. The voice gives me absolutely everything. Usually it starts with the first line and gives me the whole thrust of the plot. Once I have that, then it goes relatively quickly. Two years after that.

**AB:** Was there any particular episode or exchange that helped unlock that for you?

**MM:** I always go back to Homer and pick out the details that speak to me, and I allow my imagination to work on them. One of them was this detail that Homer gives us about Circe, where he calls her the dread goddess who speaks like a human. He just says it and moves on. But that's fascinating to think about as a novelist. What does it mean to be born as a goddess, but to have this piece of you that somehow belongs to, or is yearning for, the world of humans? In my imagination, it sets her up as a character who's trapped between worlds, who's a little bit of an outcast in both, and is trying to navigate this middle area. Those characters are always wonderful to work with because they have very interesting perspectives on both sides. So that detail, literally one word in the Greek, became a huge part of the architecture of the novel.

**AB:** It also makes her a very appropriate character for the kind of novel you're writing. Writing *Circe* from a first-person perspective is inevitably going to humanise her to your readers. So I'm fascinated to hear you say that she is the kind of God that exists between these two conditions because that makes her, in some way, particularly suited to this kind of treatment.

**MM:** There are only four myths about Circe that I had to work with. With *The Song of Achilles* I had so many stories about Achilles. You can't possibly include them all. So it was more a discarding process. But with Circe, one of the episodes that we have is told in Ovid, and it's a story of a love triangle between her and Glaucus, this god who used to be a mortal, and a nymph whose name I won't say, because it's a little bit of a spoiler . . . even though it is a 3,000-year-old story! But Ovid says something interesting about Circe. He describes her as having an *ingenium*, an inborn temperament, more fitted for love than other gods. He's referring to romantic love. But I took that to be something more like empathy. And to me, although I don't think Ovid intended this to be a reference back to Homer, those two things mapped right on to each other because I think empathy is the great gift of humanity, and it's the great gift of literature. When we read books we're experiencing someone else's life from the inside. So that was an incredibly important piece of her character for me.

**AB:** My question about whether there was a particular episode that unlocked her voice was, I think, a loaded one from my perspective. There was one moment in the book where I suddenly got a sense of who Circe is. And that's her interaction with Prometheus. I have a particular affection for Prometheus anyway – I've always found him one of the most compelling characters in Greek mythology. So perhaps first you could tell us about that exchange that they have.

**MM:** In general, if you know the Greek mythology, you know that the Greek gods are absolutely horrendous. They are cruel and selfish. They hold grudges for eternity. If you offend them, they will punish you and your children and your children's children. Today we would call them sociopathic narcissists. But there are a few exceptions to that, and Prometheus is one of them. He also has a connection to humanity. He's the god who brings fire – and, in some versions of the story, civilisation – to mankind, when Zeus is going to leave us all shivering in the caves. One of the things that I wanted to be careful about with this novel is that I did not want this to become a *Forrest Gump* of Greek literature, where Circe meets Pegasus, and then Hercules and then, you know, every major figure. So I tried to think about interactions she could have that were organic, that were suggested by the material. Her father, Helios, and her grandfather Oceanos are important pieces of the Prometheus myth. So I felt like there was a real opening there for her to connect. One of the things that I love about these stories is that – six-headed monsters and gods aside – *The Odyssey* is really the story of an exhausted war veteran trying to get home to his family and then trying to readjust to being home after twenty years of brutality. So what I wanted to do there is have her connect with someone else who can feel that kind of empathy. She's been born into this abusive family. She doesn't belong, but she doesn't really know what to do with that feeling. Sometimes an encounter with someone else can help to open a new path. So he was a very significant figure for me.

**AB:** He seemed to awaken this spirit of rebellion within her, which becomes a very important thread throughout the book. You talked about seeing what kind of exchanges the material suggested. I'm generally not very good at retaining what's considered canonical. So I started wondering about your loyalty or otherwise to the material. Novelists are known to play fast and loose with the truth and research. And yet, because you're working with something so established, how did you navigate between those two positions?

**MM:** This was something I sweated over a lot when I was working on *The Song of Achilles*, partially because it was my first time working with the classical material as a writer. I was a classicist and my mentors were classicists, and I didn't tell them I was working on it because I was afraid they were going to kick me out of the club. There were moments where I had to change things for the narrative, and it always made me very nervous. Then I had a turning point. There is a scene in *The Song of Achilles* where I finally catch up with *The Iliad*. The first scene of *The Iliad* is this huge fight between Achilles, the best warrior of the Greeks, and Agamemnon, the over-General of the Greeks. It's a sort of 'you're not the boss of me' fight. Achilles wants to kill Agamemnon, and Athena grabs him by the back of the hair and prevents him from doing it. And I could not make Athena work in that scene. She just didn't fit. Homer's words were in my head, and I felt like I was constantly fighting Homer. I couldn't find my version. I did about fifty drafts of that scene before I finally gave myself permission to cut Athena. And as soon as she was gone, I knew how to write the scene. Seeing that was a breakthrough. So by the time I was working on *Circe*, I felt a lot more freedom. And in fact, the impulse in writing *Circe* was to explicitly overturn the mythology. With *The Song of Achilles* I saw myself as bringing something to light that had always been there. But with *Circe*, I felt like I was contradicting what the material was telling us. One of the initial impulses of the book was in the confrontation with Odysseus. She goes from this powerful witch who's turning men into pigs, to suddenly dropping to her knees and begging for mercy, and inviting him into her bed, after he pulls his sword on her. The first time I read that scene I was thirteen, and it made me furious. I didn't like the kneeling and the phallic sword. I mean, it was all incredibly loaded. So I knew when I got to that scene there was going to be no kneeling. And because of my experience with Achilles, I had more confidence to say, 'no, I can push back'. That said, I do like to stay fairly close to the material because I like to talk to it. If you're adapting a text, it actually does not matter how close or how far you are in terms of how successful you will be. I always think of the movie *Clueless* as a great example of a pretty faraway adaptation. It stands on its own, but also is adapting Jane Austen's *Emma* and ends up reflecting back on the original in some interesting ways. So fidelity doesn't inherently matter. But I do like to write close because then I can feel like there are specific things I'm pushing back on and specific things I'm trying to bring out.

**AB:** On the subject of writing close: if you were adapting something like *Emma* it would be one story written by one person at one particular point. But isn't there kind of a built-in fluidity to the myths? Even though we have the sources, we also have the way they've been told and retold over the centuries. Was that liberating in a sense?

**MM:** Yes, it absolutely was. And that was what I came to understand in my fears that my classics peers were going to be upset with me. Those fears were silly, because there is no such thing as a definitive myth. We can talk about Homer's version or Ovid's version, or James Joyce's version or Margaret Atwood's version or Derek Walcott's version. All these different versions and they're all wonderful. And that was one thing that I wanted to always impress upon my classics students. That if you hear a version of the myth, you can't really say, well, that's not the right version. It may not appeal to you, but it's all out there. These stories came out of oral tradition. They were improvisational from the very beginning. So that does give us freedom where I feel like I can take what I want and discard what I don't.

**AB:** You said that the idea for the book came about as a response to the way Odysseus speaks about Circe. One of the shorthand ways for referring to this book has been to call it a feminist slant on *The Odyssey*. Before reading I wondered how that dynamic was going to work, given we have a relationship between Circe, a goddess, and Odysseus, a mortal. So there's a power dynamic which is not necessarily reflected in the dynamic between mortal men and women. And then we have the other gods. So there's this strange hierarchy. Was it a challenge approaching this multi-layered story from a feminist perspective?

**MM:** Yes. The ancient Greek gods are incredibly hierarchical. You have Zeus, and you have Helios and Poseidon and Athena and Hera, and they're up at the top, and they can pretty much do whatever they want. Every now and then the Fates will get in their way, but otherwise they can have what they want. Then there are all these ranks below that, the winds and the river gods, and all the way down at the very bottom, that's where you have nymphs. They're so low that they're almost human. If you read the mythology, particularly Ovid, the nymphs are the ones who are raped and abused and given away to husbands they don't want to marry. Their stories are really horrifying to read. They don't have any agency or control over their lives. So that was something I wanted to work with in *Circe*. She's born a goddess, which sounds great on the surface, but suddenly you realise that actually she has almost no power and she's completely at the mercy of all these gods around her. How do we get from that to this witch living by herself on an island turning men into pigs? How does that happen? Why does it happen? One of the things I loved about Circe is that witchcraft is really distinct from divinity. Divinity is what she's born to, but she becomes a witch. She makes herself a witch. She literally invents witchcraft. She's one of the first witches in ancient literature.

**AB:** 'Nymph' and 'witch' are so loaded in our culture and have been over the centuries. Whether through the witch trials, or words like nymphomaniac. But there seems to be a sort of linguistic reclaiming in your work.

**MM:** One of the things that I would advise everyone not to do is to take any female politician from any part of the political spectrum and put their name and 'witch' into Google; you will go down a horrible rabbit hole. It was shocking to me how much that word still has potency, how much we still use it as a slur against women who have more power than we think they should have, because that's really what it means. A witch is a woman with an amount of power that makes the people around her uncomfortable – that is uncontrollable by the people around her. So it was important for me to situate her within that long history of literary witches. Along with mythology, I did a lot of thinking about witches and how she fit in. You can see in the portrait of her in *The Odyssey* that she does have a lot of these proto-witchy attributes. She has a relationship to lions and wolves, animal familiars. She has the staff that she brandishes when she casts her spells. Scholars debate whether or not she's using it as sort of a 'shazam' or whether she's just using it to drive the pigs. I actually think she's just driving the pigs, but she does have it. And then there's also her connection to herbs, potions, poisons – *pharmaka* in the Greek – which are how she creates her spells. It was very interesting to study that history and to realise how resonant that word still was.

**AB:** Would both of these words have carried similar negative connotations in the Greek? You talked about the nymphs being the lowest in the hierarchy of the gods. Is that something which has been almost unbroken between ancient Greece and now?

**MM:** Absolutely. I always think it's interesting to see visual portraits of nymphs. They're a favourite subject in art throughout the centuries – beautiful naked women all hanging out together. But oftentimes their expressions are completely vacant, and their bodies are twisted in ways that are opposed to how you might naturally sit or stand. They're the passive object. That is some of what I felt Odysseus was doing to Circe. He talks about her beautiful hair as if she has prom hair, as if all she does is hang out on her island waiting for some guy to show up. That's an incredibly reductive, objectifying way to look at her. And it really fits in with that visual history of nymphs.

**AB:** When she's first going to collect the herbs to cast a spell she says, 'I stepped into those woods and my life began'. There is a sense that she is embracing these taboo powers, coming to realise herself.

**MM:** Yes. A really significant part of the novel for me was her solitude on that island, very much in the tradition of Virginia Woolf in *A Room of One's Own*. It is only by her exile and stepping away from her family that she is able to find her voice and to shed the constraints of society. But it also represents the price she has to pay. She can be independent as long as she is on this island alone. Exile ends up being a really positive thing for her.

**AB:** Although being alone also makes her incredibly vulnerable. That's a line which is trod throughout the book, the balance between her power and capacities, but also just the physical vulnerability of a woman isolated.

**MM:** Yes. And a woman alone in the ancient world was a target.

**AB:** My reintroduction to the Greek myths as an adult was through Joseph Campbell and *The Hero with a Thousand Faces*. In this book, he's quite prescriptive about the so-called hero's journey. There are these stages that every hero's quest broadly is seen to go through.

Reading *Circe* highlighted how that was a very masculine interpretation of the universal story. It really came home to me as the story advanced – and it should have been obvious from the start, really – that there is a completely different way to tell a story, and that this, let's say, more feminine narrative has always been suppressed in the telling of these myths.

**MM:** Yes. First of all there's a long history of women who wanted to study the classics not actually being allowed to work on the epics, but being pushed into art history or love poetry, the so-called softer parts, because the epics were the marquee texts, the most exciting and important. Mostly it was jealousy – male scholars keeping the most prestigious things for themselves – but also, the epics are very rooted in traditionally ancient male experience, and there was this sense that women were too delicate for all that death and war and vengeance, stuff that was associated with men. Obviously that is absurd, since plenty of women are doing the dying and avenging too, and thankfully that perspective has changed. My mentors were incredibly supportive of me pursuing epic. But also, you are right, I wanted to reclaim epic for women. I wanted to take Circe and put her at the centre, give her the same kind of scope that Achilles and Odysseus have had by right for millennia. Gods and monsters and terrible mistakes, courage and folly. At the same time, I wanted to honour the parts of ancient women's lives that have been considered not important enough for the epic. So things like craft, weaving, gardening, childbirth. That was one of the most important things for me, childbirth and parenting. In my opinion, childbirth is actually one of the most epic experiences out there. Whether you've done it yourself or supported someone through it, this is a life-changing, high-stakes experience. It should be all over epics. But because it is traditionally female it was kept out of that. So it was very important for me to have birth scenes in the novel, in particular. Also, as a writer, if you have the opportunity to write a minotaur C-section scene, you pretty much have to take it. So I did. But it was to honour that part of her journey in the mythology – to give that its importance – which is not in any of these traditional male stories.

**AB:** In bringing that to the centre, it also brings more attention to the concept of the family as well. For the most part in this book, families don't come out of it particularly well. Most are quite poisonous. Is that something you think was inherent to the way the specific families are presented in Greek mythology? Or is it something more universal to this very rigidly structured concept of the family?

**MM:** Well, the Greeks definitely knew how to do dysfunctional families. Circe's family is so wildly dysfunctional because they are gods, which means they are lacking in basic empathy, emotional skills. But I also wanted to think about people who are not born into families where they can find a home. So much of *The Odyssey* is about searching for home. Odysseus's longing for his home and homecoming – *nostos* – animates the entire epic. I wanted Circe to have that same longing. But what happens if you have this longing for home and you don't have Ithaca waiting for you? You're in flight from your family but where are you in flight to? So first Circe has to define what a good family might look like, and then create it for herself. It was also fun to work with Odysseus's family. It was exciting for me to know that Penelope was waiting for me in the last quarter of the novel. In *The Odyssey* there's all this talk about Telemachus being Odysseus's son, and how much he looks like Odysseus, and how he's going to take his father's place. He's going to uphold the line. But what always strikes me when I'm reading *The Odyssey* is that he doesn't know Odysseus at all. Odysseus has been gone for his entire life. And the person he's going to resemble, if he's going to resemble anyone, is his mother. So I was really interested in this strong mother–son relationship, and also in Circe's relationship with her son and how she's trying to do better than her parents did.

**AB:** Without saying too much about Telemachus, I think there was something about the direction you take him which is again a demonstration of how the breakdown of these imposed structures of men's roles and women's roles benefits everybody involved.

**MM:** Yes, exactly. In a society that is suppressing 50 per cent of the population, it's not just going to be 50 per cent. It's going to be everyone suffering from these constricted roles and too-narrow paths.

# Miriam Toews

*Women Talking*

Tuesday 18th June 2019

~

**Adam Biles:** In a remote Mennonite community, a group of men have been raping women, blaming the attacks on demons. The rapists have been arrested, but will be bailed in only a few days. Recognising the threat the men's return represents, a group of women meet in a hayloft to discuss how best to protect themselves. What follows is a conversation that is urgent and fraught, but also lively and galvanising as these eight women find their voices. Please join me in welcoming Miriam Toews to Shakespeare and Company.

**MT:** Thank you so much.

**AB:** It's possible that people who haven't read the book might not be aware of who the Mennonites are. Could you begin by giving us a little introduction to this quite particular group of people?

**MT:** Certainly. There are so many versions. The short, the long, the very long . . . Similar to the Amish, Mennonites started as a breakaway group from the Catholics in the 1500s in northern Holland. Since then they have a history of constant movement and migration. The central tenets are pacifism, adult baptism and communal living. One of the main mottos is 'In the world but not of the world'. There are many different ways of being a Mennonite. For instance, I live in a city and I'm educated and I'm a secular Mennonite. I was a member of the Church. I was baptised as a fifteen-year-old, which they consider to be the age of adulthood. I was excommunicated in my early twenties. I come from the first Mennonite settlement in Canada. My group came from Russia. This is a very conservative, rural-based, religious, patriarchal, authoritarian, fundamentalist community. The Mennonites of the Manitoba colony, which are the Mennonites in the book, and the place where the real crimes occurred, made the same migration from Holland to Prussia to Russia to Manitoba, where I'm from. Then this group, like so many other groups, broke away and went further afield. First to Mexico, then to Bolivia. They are always in search of a place where they can practise their religion and be 'off the grid', as they say. Different governments will sell or even give land to the Mennonites, knowing that they're for the most part good farmers, they can contribute to the economy, etc., etc. They'll stay out of trouble. So these are self-policed, self-governed communities.

**AB:** When you heard about the crimes from which this book is imagined, did you know at once that you would write about it? Did you feel your background allowed you a greater access to writing about it, or was it the reverse? That because of that proximity it would have been quite a frightening undertaking?

**MT:** The first. When I first heard about the rapes in 2009 I was horrified like everybody else. I wasn't surprised, knowing what I know of these communities. Instead of frightening me it fuelled my ongoing rage and incredulity towards my own community. In particular, the rigidity of the patriarchal structure, the lack of genuine loving forgiveness and tolerance – which is what is preached – is something I have been acutely aware of. I've said many times that

I seem to have a perpetual adolescent relationship with my own community; I'm constantly calling out the hypocrisy and violence that occurs there, not just physically and not just related to girls and women, but to boys and men as well. And the violence to the psyche. Yet, at the same time, I still have this longing to be welcomed back. Not that I would go back. I just want to be welcomed back. It's immature, but it seems not to go away. So when I heard about these crimes, I thought, 'This is something that I want to think about more. I want to create something with it.' I just didn't know exactly how I would do it.

**AB:** That 'how' was going to be my next question. The book is formally very interesting. It's the minutes of several extended meetings of these eight women. Their conversations are documented by August, a male member of their community. I'm curious about how you arrived at that particular structure.

**MT:** I thought about it for a long time. At first I had ideas of writing some kind of revenge story and then realised that I'm really not a vengeful person, so it didn't make any sense. It wouldn't make any sense with these characters. I also wanted the women to have a conversation about it. I didn't want to recreate the rapes themselves. I wanted it to be during the aftermath. I wanted an urgency to it. So a short time – forty-eight hours. Then it sort of came to me gradually that there would have to be a male narrator if I was being true to the place. Because the girls and women are illiterate in these conservative colonies. For them to be taking minutes, as it were, a male would have to do it. The male narrator is August and he's also a disenfranchised Mennonite. He's considered a half man. He's not a farmer, he's not strong. His sexuality is questioned. He was thrown out of the colony along with his family. Ona, one of the women talking, and August have always loved each other. He's come back to the colony and she senses that he's very troubled, he's despairing, he's suicidal. As an act of compassion she says to him, 'August, just come with us to the loft. We're going to be talking. We have something to work out. You've had a fancy education in England. You can write the notes.' Basically she's giving him this task that to the women is irrelevant. But it allows him to bear witness to what the women are saying. So it's an inversion really. The women are the philosophers and the thinkers and the doers and the planners. And he is the secretary, essentially. In the end, the minutes don't matter anyway. The women can't read them and they have more important things to do. The hope is that the women will go on to write their own stories and that August will, in his role as a teacher, begin to take what he's learned from the women in the loft and re-educate the boys. This is all in my head, after the book ends.

**AB:** When one reads about oppressive communities, and particularly when women are uneducated and illiterate, I think unfortunately we tend to project a lack of sophistication on to their thought. One thing that is clear immediately is that the women might not be able to write, and they might not have the specific terms, but they have the reason and the means to arrive at very complex, sophisticated philosophical conclusions. This was something you were keen to get across right from the beginning, and to overturn our preconceptions.

**MT:** Absolutely. It was certainly a challenge – given their collective very limited experience in the world – for them to have this discussion, which is theological, philosophical, and which all takes place within the context of their faith, which was also important to them and for me to get across. August can interpret some of the stuff using language that he would be familiar with – 'patriarchy' or 'commodity' or these types of things. Concepts that the women just wouldn't have. But like you say, they have the reasoning, just without the specific language. There's also the idea of language as a revolutionary tool. Language is powerful and oppressive at times, especially in the fundamentalist interpretation of the Bible, and the misogyny inherent in that. It was important for me to show that these women are real. They tease each other, they attack each other. They argue, they are subversive, they mourn, they cry, they contradict themselves. They fight. And because the perception of Mennonites is similar to Amish – this crazy, cultish, backward, medieval group of religious freaks – I wanted to alter that and show that these are human beings with urgency and agency, but also humanity.

**AB:** What comes across really distinctly is the intergenerational relationships. We see teenagers acting like any other teenager. Then you have the mothers and grandmothers and the dynamic between the three generations. Seeing the same rhythms and dynamics playing out in their lives was really effective at closing that gap between us and this religious community.

**MT:** Writing the teenage girls was a lot of fun, while always bearing in mind the pain and trauma that they're embodying. But to be a teenager in this context where there are women talking about these very important subjects, the opportunity for mockery, sarcasm, boredom, for their crushes on the various boys in the community and their own lives and their own friendships . . . all of that stuff was fun to write. It was a break for me as the writer. And maybe it is a little bit of a break from the intensity of the conversation.

**AB:** From the ambient intensity of the events as well. You said that you don't describe the attacks at all, but there are occasional punctual references to them. There is an air of, not a parable exactly, but a story a bit out of time. Then you drop in these references, none of them graphic, to some of the crimes and it brings the reader up short and reminds us of the brutality of what went on. How did you negotiate that violence in the writing?

**MT:** It was with the rhythm and the pacing. Within the conversation there are moments of, I suppose, levity. There are jokes and humorous stuff. But these things have happened to them and they're there for a reason. So it was important to always have that inside myself as well. I'd have the teenagers fooling around in a funny way and then have to include a reminder that, for instance, the three-year-old daughter of one of the women has a venereal disease, and one of the older women has a badly fitting set of false teeth because hers were smashed right out of her mouth.

**AB:** As a reader it grounds you in a profound way. Early in the conversation, the women come up with three options: do nothing, stay and fight, or leave. This is a very specific discussion about a specific set of circumstances, and yet 'do nothing', 'stay and fight' and 'leave' seem to be three options which apply to almost every situation of oppression.

**MT:** The stakes are high for each one of them. They're all fraught, uncertain, dangerous options. It's not an easy decision to make. In any oppressive situation that we find ourselves, or any uncomfortable situation, or where we're unhappy – what should we do? Do we stay at a job, in a marriage, in university? It's stuff that we're all grappling with almost all the time.

**AB:** And then unpicking whether there's a difference between leaving and fleeing? Is leaving a surrender? Is it a show of weakness or a show of strength?

**MT:** Yeah. They're very concerned about language, about the difference in these words. Are we leaving or are we fleeing? Are we running away like a terrified animal, or are we making a conscious choice to leave? This is important.

**AB:** Concerning language, one thing I don't think we have said is that as well as documenting the conversation August Epp is also translating it. The women are talking in Plattdeutsch, and August is listening and then translating it into English. Earlier you said language could be liberating or it could be very constraining. Is this a language which has remained relatively static since the foundation of the colony, or is it one which has evolved?

**MT:** I don't think it has evolved from what people who are more informed tell me. It's a dying language. It's a language that only Mennonites speak, really. My mother still speaks it with her older Mennonite friends. My sister spoke it a little bit and I don't really speak it at all. My parents, like so many Mennonite parents who are a little bit more liberal, didn't want us to learn the language. There was even that understanding in my parents' generation that even though they might not be in the world, our generation would need to be. It's also an unwritten language. It is the language of these women in the book, the women in real life in these closed colonies. They don't speak the language of the country that they're in. As the language is unwritten, this means they're illiterate. So they are virtual prisoners. They really are held hostage in these places. They don't leave the colonies without being accompanied by a man, a brother or husband or whatever. When these types of crimes occur, there's no recourse. There's nowhere for them to go. There's no way that they can ask for help.

**AB:** August, who has lived out, provides the word 'patriarchy'. That was a very resonant moment because they are describing something which the language doesn't have a word for. It raises the question about how much one is able to imagine a concept, to understand a concept if one isn't able to name it.

**MT:** Right. They talk about the Bible in that way too: 'We've been told by the male leaders in the community, that this is what it says in the Bible.' Because, of course, it is always translated or interpreted by the men in a way that benefits the men. Slowly, over time, this dehumanises the women. The women talk about this, and they say, 'Well, how do we really know that's what it says in the Bible?' But what's so threatening about this book, specifically, is that these women are talking, and in a way creating their own religion, extrapolating from the old, with all of the beautiful aspects of the Mennonite faith and of many faiths – love, compassion, tolerance – and trying to create something where they can engage and be safe, and genuinely worship.

**AB:** One of the specific areas they take issue with is the idea of forgiveness. There's a moment where you write that the women 'will be given the opportunity to forgive these men, thus guaranteeing everyone's place in heaven'. Structurally, this idea of forgiveness has been twisted to benefit the men.

**MT:** It's a Mennonite version of restorative justice in that, when something like this happens – and this, of course, is an extremely horrific, egregious crime, but it applies to lesser crimes too – the idea is that the perpetrator of the crime says, 'I did this, I'm sorry, will you forgive me?' and the person that was violated says, 'Yes, I forgive you' and that's it. The concept of forgiveness is a beautiful thing. I believe in forgiveness. But in this context, it doesn't work because what happens is that these things continue to go on and on and on, and the root causes are never examined or changed. The women are basically, once again, silenced. This sounds like some sort of hyperbole but this is the reality in these communities.

**AB:** Which brings us back to the idea of staying and fighting or leaving. Because staying and fighting only has value if you think there is something which can actually be fought. If the structures are so deeply rooted, if there's no way that they can be demolished, then you're not left with any option. You have to leave and rebuild from scratch as much as possible.

**MT:** Absolutely. It's a type of war that the women are engaged in with the men in their community, men who are related to them, men who they often love and fear at the same time. When that's the case, and you have no weapons, no arsenal of your own, what do you do?

**AB:** When the women are considering leaving, there's this repeated question of where will we go, how will we know where we're going? The subject of maps comes up quite a lot. They don't have maps, but there's a possibility that they might be able to find a map, although they're not sure if they're going to be able to read the map. When you're trying to create something new, you have the familiarity of the structures that are holding you back, or you have the great unknown, which can be both terrifying and liberating.

**MT:** Exactly. Again, for the teenagers, it's like, 'all right, let's go'. The others are, of course, more pragmatic and thinking of all of the various logistics involved in staying or leaving. The map thing came from a little anecdote told to me by my mother, who really has her ear to the ground when it comes to the Mennonite grapevine. A friend of hers had been to this specific colony, the Manitoba in Bolivia. The teacher in the colony said, 'It'd be so nice if we had a world map.' I was struck by the enormity of that. Not knowing where you are in the world. And that's a teacher in a school saying this. All my life, and in all my work, there has been this longing for the world, which is like a drug when you're a Mennonite and you're stuck in one of these communities. The world can be so beautiful and joyful and fun and inspiring and edifying in all sorts of ways. As a Mennonite, I inhabit that limbo, that liminal space of not belonging in my community, but also not belonging in the world.

**AB:** With the older generations there's this fear that has been inculcated about what the world could do to them, how the world will treat them. Is that something which develops with age in these communities? Is it intentionally inculcated or is it more a sort of natural conservatism?

**MT:** It could be both. My own mother was always wanting to go, but she was committed to my father in a very traditional Mennonite fashion. When he died she left the community. She had longed to leave the community from a very early age, and up until the moment that she left in her sixties the desire to leave only got stronger. But I know other people, friends and family who have stayed in the community, don't really understand what it is that I am hoping for or enjoying out here. They want to stay and they know that's where they will stay, whether they feel they belong there or not.

**AB:** A lot of it seems to ultimately come down to the stories we tell each other, the stories we tell about ourselves. One of the ways in which sophisticated ideas are communicated in their conversation seems to be through little stories, little parables. Is that something which comes quite naturally to Mennonite language and culture? It may not have evolved beyond a certain point but has adapted in other ways?

**MT:** I think so. Also, their familiarity, our familiarity, with the Bible and its many stories and its many metaphors. It's a natural extension to describe our lives in the same way. Particularly in the remote

Mennonite communities, it's natural to tell stories about nature, with animals or skies or weather or crops, because that's their world.

**AB:** At one moment, August remembers his father describing the twin pillars that guard the entrance to the shrine of religion as 'storytelling' and 'cruelty'. This really interested me, particularly connected to something you said earlier about the women creating their own religion. Is that something which you broadly share, that these are the twin pillars of religion, or is there potential in the action these women are taking to reinvent religion with other pillars?

**MT:** There's always potential to reinvent religion with other pillars. But I feel at this point that those are the two pillars of religion. I mean, we can see that. Within that, of course, is the idea of faith, of hope and of thinking of oneself living your life as Jesus would, with humility, with kindness, and with compassion and selflessness. It's not black and white. I'm hopeful that something will change . . . but maybe the world will come to an end before we actually get there.

**AB:** I'd like to talk about the subject of re-educating and re-founding. Something that the women run up against in their conversation is what to do about the men and boys. The men of a certain generation, we almost get the sense they're a lost cause. There is a moment where one of the characters says, 'well, are they also just not as much victims as us?' which provokes discussion. But there's a lot of time spent deciding what to do about the boys, particularly boys approaching adolescence from about twelve to fifteen. That seems to be something which is more broadly relevant as well, beyond this community. That question of who is responsible for educating boys differently?

**MT:** The women grapple with that. Many of them have sons and brothers. If they do decide to leave, the question is 'who will come with us?'. Where's the cut off? If they're fifteen, they're baptised in the community and they are considered to be full members of the Church with the right to have some kind of say in the colony. And how do you convince a fifteen-year-old boy to come with you? It's painful. Everything is just so fraught. The urgency of them attempting to keep their children safe, to prevent their children – their daughters, especially, but their sons, too – from being harmed, systemically and systematically. These crimes are real. They are continuing to happen, even though the original perpetrators are behind bars. Now more than ever the push is on. The women are desperate. It's one thing to forcibly take your young children with you – because that's what we do, we take our young children with us where we go. But with an adolescent, it's not as easy.

**AB:** In the end, there are no easy answers. The book doesn't try to provide them either. I'd like to conclude with the title. It's so simple, so elegant, and so forceful. Was it always clear to you that the book would be called *Women Talking*?

**MT:** It wasn't my first title. I had some others. Titles are hard. But I like the title because, when people say to me, 'Well, it's just women talking. I mean, that's all. Nothing really happens', I say, 'Yeah, but you were warned.' I really wasn't aware of the threat that women talking represents to certain people – in my own community, but also the community at large. The idea of a group of women getting together, not even secretly. What are you talking about? What are you plotting? What kind of rebellion? I think this book specifically struck fear into the hearts of that group of Mennonite elders that always hates what I do. But this time it was really an attempt to discredit me, saying, 'How can you write this way about Mennonites?

Showing them to be such animals, so violent? How can you show that part of Mennonites?' There was never any mention from these same men of how these women are being portrayed with agency, with a voice, attempting to determine for themselves what is going on in their lives. But they're Mennonites, too. So when they say, 'How can you show Mennonites in this light?' they're talking about men. It's irrelevant what Mennonite women are being portrayed as or how they are being shown to the world. They're interested in having the world see them, us, as this very simple, harmonious, loving, peaceful, hard-working group of people with strong faith. But it's amazing to me, I'm just learning this now at my advanced age, how threatening that is. A group of women just getting together and talking.

# Katie Kitamura

*Intimacies*

Thursday 8th July 2021

~

**Adam Biles:** The narrator of *Intimacies*, Katie Kitamura's enthralling fourth novel, is an interpreter who moves to The Hague to take up a post at the International Criminal Court. To begin with she wonders if the move might also mark the end to her, so far, rootless life, but soon begins questioning whether her vocation forbids such an existence. For while the role of the interpreter is to bridge the fissures between language, it also offers the temptation to stare down into those fissures at the seething abyss of human contradictions beneath. Indeed, *Intimacies* is a book that embodies these very contradictions, a feat of literary alchemy that testifies to Kitamura's extraordinary skill as a novelist. Please welcome Katie Kitamura to Shakespeare and Company.

**Katie Kitamura:** Thank you.

**AB:** I have a feeling with your last two novels, *Intimacies* and *A Separation*, that in a way they begin almost before most novels begin. By which I mean they begin with the title. That may seem like a strange thing to say, but my feeling is that titles are often ambiguous, and only take on meaning as you progress through the book, sometimes only near the end of the book, or sometimes not at all. Whereas I think what you did with *A Separation* and do again with *Intimacies* is you present readers with a concept that perhaps feels quite familiar to us. And then you take that idea, and you sort of unpack it through your characters, through the stories of their lives. So I'm curious to know if that is how the novels come to you, if you begin with an idea to explore and then start unpacking it, or rather if that idea crystallises in the writing.

**KK:** In the case of *Intimacies* we actually changed the title at the last minute. I don't know if you've had this experience of trying to find a title. I just took a literal envelope and wrote down a list of words. And that's how we ultimately came upon *Intimacies*. I do think the titles are important with *A Separation* and *Intimacies*, because the voices of the two books are quite similar in a lot of ways. But to me the books are almost diametrically opposed in that *A Separation* is about a woman who starts off thinking she understands the story of her life, and then by the end of the book understands that, after all, she doesn't. I think *Intimacies* is something different. It's about pieces falling into place. It's about closeness, the potential for resolution. I think in that sense, the titles certainly do represent something thematically central to the books.

In terms of where I started with this particular book, it was with the subjective position of an observer. This idea of observation and the point at which that tips over into voyeurism. I was really interested in thinking about how a character might then step forward into their life. Is that possible when you've become so accustomed to thinking of yourself as an observer at the margins? I think that position is compelling to me for a lot of reasons. I was interested in questions of complicity and implication, to what extent calling yourself an observer is to grant yourself a neutrality that is maybe offering a kind of ethical cover. And the position of an observer is also not too far from the position of a writer. The question of where the writer chooses to place themselves – always, but particularly in the last four or five years – is something certainly that I've been thinking about.

**AB:** That role of the interpreter is fascinating because they are somebody, as you say, who's very present in a scene – so at the International Criminal Court you have these benches full of interpreters – and yet their role is almost to erase themselves. The perfect interpreter almost wouldn't be noticed at all, they would just facilitate a seamless interaction between two people speaking different languages. How did you think yourself into the mind of an interpreter? Did you actually have to go out and meet with people who occupy that role or was it an act of pure imagination?

**KK:** Thematically I was very interested in interpretation and translation, in the idea of characters that language passes through and what that means. What it means to be a conduit for languages. I think in this book in particular, I was thinking about how language, even as it passes through you, leaves a trace, and how it's very hard not to be changed by the language that you speak, and also not to change the language that you speak. In practical terms, I did interview several interpreters who worked at the International Criminal Court, who were hugely useful. Probably the biggest surprise for me was that I thought that they would be almost self-effacing in some way, because of the nature of their work. That they would be relatively quiet or somehow austere in their personality. Instead they were remarkably charismatic. They were very good at performing because, as they pointed out to me, their job is not simply to speak the words, but also to perform them and to give them meaning that is not necessarily communicated just through the literal meaning of the word. Irony, for example, or humour. You need to be able to communicate that in the way that you interpret.

The other thing that I was interested in was this very obvious fact – that language comes from somewhere. And often it comes from, and is shaped by, institutions. In this case, it's shaped by the huge institution of the justice system. So I definitely wanted to think about how perceptions of neutrality would play into that.

**AB:** One of the things that I hadn't really considered before was the physical presence of the interpreter. So there are two different modes of interpretation presented in the book. There's the one in which the interpreters are in a booth detached from the action. They're there, but they're not there. They're somewhere between participants and spectators in the court. But there are also several scenes in which your narrator interprets live, whispering directly into the ear of one particular character. And it really struck me that here they are acting both as an intellectual conduit, while also assuming a physical presence. I can only imagine how draining it must be to channel all of this meaning from one person to another.

**KK:** I think this returns to your very first question about the title. One thing that I realised after I finished the book and before I chose the title was that 'intimacy' as a word seems to connote security or safety. It has certain associations of warmth, or love, or eroticism. But of course, it can also be a form of violence. There are a lot of instances in the book of sexual intimidation and sexual harassment and – what you're speaking about – that kind of phys-ical and psychological intimacy that can feel uneasy, particularly when we're thrust into it without warning. It was definitely some-thing that played into those scenes. They're also two very, very different modes of interpretation. In the context of a tribunal you're really speaking into a historical record. The other is very intimate. You're speaking to one person, and you're speaking for one person. Navigating that gap between those two kinds of communication was really interesting for me to think about.

One thing that I think the novel is really about, and which comes from my own experience, is the question of what it means to be an individual as these larger historic events are taking place around you, and how you reconcile that gap between the centrality and importance of what you know is happening around you, and your very stupid, petty, everyday concerns. Like, did I buy milk? Or maybe I'm irritated my partner didn't unload the dishwasher. The scale of emotion is very hard to manage. I wanted the book to go from the very small scale, interpreting for one person alone, to something that was much bigger and almost beyond the scope of what the individual can actually perceive. The narrator often only has access to fragments of information. She only has little shards. She never has the big picture. That felt to me a little bit like what it's like trying to pass through a historically significant moment. All the time I feel like I'm trying to see the big picture, but I keep just getting little snippets here and there.

**AB:** I think one thing that's really fascinating in the novel is the effect that has on the narrator's conception of herself. It's interesting that you say the interpreters you met were often quite theatrical, quite large characters. I wonder if that's a means of defence against being subsumed by both being a conduit of information between two people, but also having to reckon with the insignificance of one's persona in this strange, much more historically significant context.

**KK:** This is why I love talking to Adam so much, because he makes me think things that I just have never thought before! I think it's so true that performance is a kind of protection. If you are a performer, then at the end of it you can say to yourself, 'that was that. And this is now my actual life.' Performance is certainly something that I'm really preoccupied with when I write fiction. The starting point for my last novel was the idea of a woman who had separated from her partner, but they hadn't told anybody. The partner dies and then she has to perform the role of a grieving spouse throughout the novel. The collapse of the persona and the individual experience is the arc the novel tracks. So here, it's the idea of the courtroom as a place of contradiction, because you think if ever there is a place where the truth matters it is in these war crime tribunals. But in reality, on the one hand we have this ideal of justice, but on the other hand there's everything that compromises justice as it is enacted in real life. These trials are incredibly theatrical. They are performances. So that contradiction was at the heart of the book. But the idea that the performance would be a form of self-preservation was not something I had thought about. But now that you say it, I see that's absolutely true.

**AB:** I'm interested in this idea of fragments of information, that you mentioned earlier. In the context of the trial of the former dictator a single fragment of evidence can still be incredibly powerful, incredibly condemnatory. And yet at other moments the former president's defence is able to reframe other fragments of evidence to present a very different story. This is something which our narrator experiences in the court, but also in her life outside. Now, I don't know if it's necessarily the experience of the court that is making her act in this way, but there's certainly the sense that the more she integrates into life in The Hague, the less she feels she has a real sense of the city she's in, the people she meets and what they mean to each other and how they interact.

**KK:** I think that's absolutely true for me. The real moment of horror in a relationship, or in a friendship, or any experience with a person, is when you look at the person that you feel you know very well and then you see a stranger. That's always a moment that's intriguing to me, and certainly this is happening to her constantly throughout the course of the novel. I actually don't know what I think of it, but I made a decision to take the central love interest of this character and remove him from the novel. So we meet him for a couple of scenes and then he leaves and only returns at the end of the book. This is a structure that I replicated in my last book as well, where the . . . I actually hate the phrase 'love interest', but you know, the person, whatever he is, the object of feeling – is not there. I've lately been wondering why that is. Why I choose to write relationships in this way and what that says about me. For me first-person is a form that I love but which has, for a very long time, been very fraught, because I always found the authority of first-person almost troubling in some way. It's so different to how I feel myself to be. I feel myself to be a person who knows and understands very little of the world. I'm not a raconteur. I'm not a storyteller in that way. I think first-person popped open for me when I realised that I could try to use it primarily as a mode of speculation. So my narrator is a character who's always hypothesising. And in her personal life, that kind of hypothesising around an absence is almost the most productive, and almost the most erotic and romantic, mode for her.

**AB:** How much of that also was connected to the location of The Hague? I feel that The Hague is quite undefined as a city compared to somewhere like New York, where the narrator lived before, and which may have multifarious meanings for different people, but which seems to have an identity that's in some way easier to pin down. It sounds a bit of a cliché, but was the city, for you, an important character in the book?

**KK:** It absolutely was. I had such a funny experience writing the book because I went to The Hague and I sat in on a trial at the ICC, and I spent about a week or two doing all the writerly stuff like finding the neighbourhood where my characters would live, doing the narrator's commute. And throughout, I felt that it was a very familiar city to me, but I didn't know exactly why. So I wrote that feeling into the novel. Then I realised, only after I'd finished the first draft, that in fact I had spent a lot of time there as a child, which I'd completely forgotten somehow. Because my father, who's an academic, would take sabbatical there and so we'd all go away as a family for several months. We did it two or three times. So there was a real familiarity to the city that I couldn't quite put my finger on while I was writing it. And then I later realised why that was. Then that became, in some ways, a kind of emotional anchor for the final section of the book, in which certain pieces start to fall into place, and the narrator is finally able to put things in their context. That was something that was directly taken from my own life. That feeling of alienation from yourself, the sense that there are things in your own history or being you cannot place. Often, you don't have the perfect record or context of these long segments of your life. But in practical terms I didn't know any of that when I started writing. I only knew that I wanted the book to be at a war crimes tribunal, and The Hague was a fairly obvious choice.

**AB:** I'm going to try and talk around it because I don't want to give too much away about what actually happens in the book, but I'm interested in this idea of the pieces falling into place, because there's a moment when a particular upcoming political event is referred to that places it at a particular date – early 2016, I guess. Because of what's happened in the world, in the UK and the US and various other countries since 2016, my sense was that *Intimacies* was going to be a novel about fragments dispersing, about things moving away from each other. And so I found this urge to bring the fragments together at the end both surprising and refreshing, in a way.

**KK:** Yes. I guess I have two thoughts about that. One is that I'm very nervous of writing the same thing again. I think I felt an anxiety about just doing what I know. I felt like I knew how to write an ending where a character would feel that sense of alienation or loneliness or whatever it might be. That's very much how I ended the last book. So even though I didn't know exactly what would be happening at the end of the book, I knew the kind of feeling I wanted it to have – which it doesn't achieve! But I knew what I was aspiring towards. I've always loved the ending of the Chekhov short story, 'The Lady with the Dog'. I think the end of that story is extraordinary because you think you know these characters and you think you understand what the fate of their relationship might be. And then in the final page or so, it's like a door opening. That to me is just one of the most magical moments in literature. When I was writing the book, I thought, 'I know how to do this sense of claustrophobia and this sense of paralysis, but I don't know if I know how to do the sense of a door opening up.' So I knew that I wanted the end of the book to have this sense of something opening up rather than closing down.

The second is that, over the last four or five years as I was writing the book, I found the urge to consolidate was very, very strong. One of the strangest things about the last four years is that it's been a period of such deep global uncertainty and unrest and unhappiness. But within my own personal life it has actually been a moment of great happiness. I have had children. I'm with a person that I love. And so reconciling that, not dismissing that feeling, was something that I wanted to try to think about in this book. It's easy to say, 'your personal happiness doesn't mean anything in a time of global crisis'. What's more difficult is the need to reconcile two opposing things. We live in a world where that contradiction exists. We live in a world where you have to grapple with that cognitive dissonance between your small life and its small happiness, and the larger things that are happening around you.

**AB:** That's fascinating because as I was reading the book, the word I wrote several times in my notes was 'home'. This idea is very preoccupying for your narrator. She feels very rootless. There's this interrogation throughout about what home means and if she has the capacity to find it. And then there's one particular moment when she has to go and interpret for an Islamist fighter who's been captured and you give us a description of his cell. You write, 'the space we gathered in was somewhere between a cell and a dormitory room with a single bed and a desk and a toilet in one corner'. And it struck me that all of the elements of a physical home, a living space, were present. Yet he was as far away from anything resembling a home as he could be. All of which is to say that I'm curious about whether that chimes with what you felt when you were writing, that she was essentially trying to take the fragments of the world and construct them into a home.

**KK:** I think the structure of the book is about grief. It starts with the fact of her father's death and doesn't return to it until the very end. I think for people who have grown up between cultures, as I very much did, the notion of home is not always located in a place, but is often located in the bodies of the people that you love. So what happens when that body is gone? That, to some extent, is the animating question, the answer she's searching for. A lot of the spaces in the novel are temporary: she's in temporary accommodation; she moves into her object-of-feeling's apartment, which is very much haunted by the ghost of his wife, or his soon-to-be-ex wife. If you don't rely on physical spaces for a sense of home, where does that leave you? It's just a different way of being, but to me the home that she finds is no less valid than the home of somebody who considers themselves to be firmly of a more bounded geographical and physical place.

# Claire-Louise Bennett

## *Checkout 19*

### Monday 6th September 2021

~

**Adam Biles:** *Checkout 19* is about reading and writing, and the presence and power of books. But it's also about class and the burning need many of us have felt to escape the life to which society tries to condemn us, tries to condemn women perhaps most of all. It's written with the astonishing combination of literary sophistication and lexical playfulness that won Claire-Louise Bennett so many fans when her debut *Pond* was released. Claire-Louise, welcome to the Shakespeare and Company podcast.

**Claire-Louise Bennett:** Hello Adam.

**AB:** I'd like to begin with the subject of memory. Or perhaps it's better to say remembering, because a lot of the book is the narrator reaching back into her past and unearthing these events, some of them very distant. This struck me as a different perspective to *Pond*, which felt more immediate. Did that feel like a fundamental shift for you?

**CLB:** With *Pond* there was a deliberate move towards focusing on the immediate. That was as a way of extricating myself from academia.

I'd been studying for a number of years and I wanted to get out of that way of thinking. I'd stopped studying, but my brain was still functioning in that very analytic, intellectual way. Which was hindering me creatively, in the long term. The stuff I was looking at during my PhD was very beneficial; concepts relating to, say, selfhood and artistic representations of the self definitely fed in. But in terms of actually writing, producing words and sentences, I needed to unravel a little bit. So focusing on the immediate was useful in that regard.

When it came time to put this book together, years had gone by since *Pond* and I was at that time in my life when I started to have a distinct sense of having a past. Up until that point, and certainly around the time I was writing *Pond*, my life had felt all of a piece. Now my past almost seems like a different lifetime. So this made me curious about past events and circumstances that I'd maybe over-emphasised, and other things that maybe I hadn't really acknowledged. For example, I've lived in Ireland for just over twenty years now and from time to time I get asked why I came here. I've always answered that facetiously or evasively. Most of the time I say I came here to get away from England. Which is true, but it doesn't explain very much. It took me a while to really think about it, because you're just getting on with it, and dealing with the repercussions of that decision. It's only recently that I've reflected on it, and then I think, 'Well, really I know I left because I didn't have much available to me in England, in terms of what I might do with my life.' Before I left the UK I'd been working in a WHSmith warehouse doing night shifts. I preferred working in warehouses to office work, because it's more physical. So I suppose things were presenting themselves to me more fully than they had done before.

I've got a very bad memory, actually. I wrote the first section many years ago. The first line of the original piece was, 'We remember our first memory don't we. Yes, yes, yes, we do. But that's not the same thing as the first thing that happened is it? No, no, no, it isn't. We don't remember what the first thing that happened is do we? No, we don't.' In that piece I was allowing for the possibility that at some point in my life I might have an earlier memory. My first memory that I have now won't always be my first memory. I hope not. I hope I manage to get an earlier one.

**AB:** It's interesting that you say you don't have a very good memory. Another writer who said the same thing was Karl Ove Knausgaard. *Checkout 19* and *My Struggle* are very different projects, but as a reader they had a similar effect on me. They plunged me back into my own memories. In excavating your past, you were allowing me to do the same. I've been trying to figure out what produces this effect and I was wondering if it had something to do with the acknowledgement of the fluidity of memory and its disintegration. Often in memoir and autobiography everything is presented as concrete and clear. Often with a defined arc or journey. Whereas in *Checkout 19*, for example, you're talking about your jacket on a chair and you say, sometimes I see a green jacket and sometimes it's purple. Did you have to fight against that expectation of solidity, and coherence, and fact, while excavating these memories? Were you tempted to concretise things when to you perhaps they weren't so concrete?

**CLB:** That's really interesting, and there's a few things to think about there. No, I knew I wasn't attempting to write a memoir, for a range of reasons. A memoir presents life in a particular kind of way. It feels like there's an inevitability to how things went in a sense. There is an almost definitive take on the significance of certain events, which I can't take on because I don't feel that certainty. So it doesn't feel appropriate to work in that mode. Also, I think it does set up a different reading experience, so I was interested in what you had to say about my book and Knausgaard's inviting this sort of participation. That's something I very much wanted to happen, and I don't think that necessarily happens when you read memoir. I enjoy memoir, it's nice sometimes to have this whole life play out in front of you. But it feels very contrived, weirdly enough. It doesn't feel particularly convincing to me because my experience of life hasn't been that way at all. I find thinking about life as a journey quite problematic – I suppose I'm more drawn to the notion of stillness or quietism and what that offers up.

**AB:** One of the areas where it had this evocative effect most strongly is when you're writing about school. One thing that set it apart is that it didn't feel as if school was a time of infinite possibility to you. Possibly because a lot of literature comes from people who went to private schools where opportunity is really stressed. One element that resonated with me was not exactly the futility of the school experience but almost like it was a joke being played on the kids. As if the teachers were going through the motions, they had things they said about your work experience or your career plan, but they didn't really believe it. And the kids didn't really believe it about themselves.

**CLB:** One thing I should say is that I didn't write it all from scratch. It came together last year during the first lockdown, which was pretty full on in Ireland. I was working with a lot of material that already existed. I didn't know as I was writing it that the school thing was going to become what it did. Things just sort of exploded. I'd had these scrappy bits for a long time and I was in London a couple of years ago trying to put them together and it just wasn't working. I don't know what it was but there was something about being stuck at home last year with these pieces that helped me get into them and bring them together.

Another thing that's always very galvanising is anger. I'd read that piece in the *Guardian* about working-class students being bullied in universities. We're talking about adults bullying other adults because of the way their voice sounds. Privileged adults making other people feel bad because . . . Ah! Even talking about it now I can feel myself getting angry. So this anger was apparent as I was writing. And it's frequently funny too. When you grow up in that kind of environment, the things that make you angry you quickly make humorous in some way as well. That's the way of dealing with stuff, right? You make it into a joke, because what else are you going to do with it except go mad? It can be really overwhelming, that feeling of injustice and inequality, I remember feeling so angry when I was about nineteen or twenty especially – though at that time I couldn't have told you why.

When I was reading over those pieces I was reminded of my own experiences and how naive I'd been. I had thought for a while, when I was at school, that if I did knuckle down I would do well. That I would be able to do something interesting with my life and that opportunities would open up. I had to believe that, to a degree, because I knew I didn't want to stay in that town, or that place. I just didn't feel particularly comfortable there, so I had to conceive of a way out.

But after a while school did feel pointless because classes were so unruly a lot of the time. After a while it does get annoying. Just not that much fucking fun. You think, 'Well I would rather be on my own.' So I don't know whether my tendency towards solitude occurred then, but I did like doing projects on my own. Then there's that awakening, because she goes off and does A-Levels at college – obviously her crud school doesn't have a sixth-form – and she realises that actually the schooling she's received so far has been pretty flimsy.

**AB:** I'm conscious that to a lot of our listeners around the world there's something mysterious about the class system in Britain, or perhaps England more specifically. Listeners in the United States, where there's the myth of the American dream, could be potentially baffled by the situation that you just outlined, this sense of being almost a prisoner of the class in which you're born. Which is not to say that there is not an escape – you and I both escaped by leaving the country – but there's something particularly English about this stratified and fixed class system, and the attitudes you provoke depending on which level of society you're born into.

**CLB:** It's so entrenched. The minute someone opens their mouth lots of unexamined assumptions are instantly and lastingly made about them. Probably a lot of people aren't even aware they're being discriminatory, it's so embedded. There are a lot of unhelpful clichés about every class I suppose. I don't know much about the working class as it's typically represented. I didn't grow up on a council estate. None of my family were on benefits or unemployed. We had quite a lot of money. We had a Volvo. My parents wore Barbour jackets in the winter when we went for walks up Marlborough Forest. From the outside, we had all the tropes of a middle-class life. But having those things doesn't make you middle class. It's not just about having the right sort of jacket or car. What you realise – and I think this is the most frustrating thing – is that it's really about professional connections and social networks and those kinds of things. It's very hard to get on in life without those.

At least I was able to go to university, because at the time you didn't have to pay fees. Plus you had a maintenance grant – although my maintenance grant was poxy. Anyway, after I graduated I went back to my hometown and it was as though I hadn't done the degree. I may as well not have done it. It didn't lead to anything. I'm the only person in my family who has a degree. No one's bothered since. It doesn't have any value without the connections, or at least some proper money behind you, because if you're lucky you might get an internship – but who can afford to do those?

**AB:** The way working-class life is typically presented is a particular bugbear of mine. Because there is almost the authorised vision of the working class. Authorised by the middle- and upper-class gate-keepers that often operate in certain sectors. The publishing industry, for example. We have this sense that if you're not from Birmingham or further north, if your family is not beset by social problems, you don't tick the boxes of being the acceptable face of the working class to the people who decide which books are going to get published. So one of the things I found refreshing about *Checkout 19* was this presentation of what people I know jokingly call the upper working class . . .

**CLB:** Ah, yeah! I think I thought that was a real term for a while . . .

**AB:** It's the kind of families who don't have university education, where the parents maybe left school at sixteen, got jobs or apprenticeships. And brought up their kids with this idea of getting on in life. They do all the things they're told they're supposed to do, they tick all the boxes they're supposed to tick, go to university – and yet, as you say, they end up back in their hometown without the fabled doors opening for them, as they'd been promised.

**CLB:** Another aspect of that is the expectation that if you are a writer from a working-class background you're going to write about working-class life, in a very realist, gritty way. I don't write like that. But there is very much an assumption that that's your world and you can't extend beyond it. That's why I found Ann Quin so powerful and interesting and inspiring. She was from a working-class background. She was brought up by her mum. She was born in Brighton, did low-paid jobs, lived in dreary bedsits and so on, yet she always had a sense of life as being almost – what's the word? – cosmic or something. She craved a different scale of existence. I remember that feeling, how intense it is – it's probably something a lot of us feel when we're younger. Then it all gets whittled down to this very narrow life path. And she wasn't up for that. I know I wasn't up for that at all. It's that desire to want to remain open and in touch with everything. That's what fuelled her. There's a lot of detail about working-class domestic environments in her novels but they're very unusual descriptions, sort of turned on their head, which led to them being compared in an unflattering way to the *nouveau roman*. At the time she was seen as being imitative of that particular genre, which was mean, and again reveals a class blind spot. Critics at the time couldn't really see that her writing was coming from an authentic place. Her work has got that phenomenological dimension to it. I just love that she goes beyond. I'm not quite sure how she does it actually.

**AB:** It's very telling that it's only really in the last few years that she's getting anything like the recognition that her talent deserved. And that's only because of the dedication and persistence of a few people. Indeed, throughout *Checkout 19* you bring in a range of books and writers and show how they've shaped you. One of these is *A Room With a View*. You don't know what to make of it at first, but then you get caught up in it and, with a few friends, make a trip to Florence to try and channel the forces that are present in that book.

**CLB:** I think there can be a tendency, as a working-class person, to have romantic ideas about literature. There's a deep contradiction in me because I can't stand systems of privilege, but I really enjoy a good costume drama at the same time. Then I get really annoyed afterwards, I'm disgusted with myself. Being a writer is fulfilling something that seems very romantic. At seventeen or so I don't think class discrepancies and discriminations were forefront in my mind. I was looking, more than anything, to understand, or feel, or inhabit very strong emotions. And literature is one of the ways that helps us do that. That particular book is so beautiful, and very funny. And again it hints at this different scale of living. It's all Beauty and Love and Courage! It's always so exciting and thrilling, isn't it, when you open a book and see those sorts of words, they hit you right between the eyes.

**AB:** Obviously *A Room with a View* and *Checkout 19* are vastly different books, and yet I think they have a kind of sincerity in common. Which I think is actually quite a difficult thing to sustain. Often books will lapse into sincerity for a short while. This sort of sustained sincerity throughout an entire 300-page book is very rare. As a writer is it quite exhausting?

**CLB:** I didn't find it exhausting at all. I found it quite energising. I think sometimes you can be a bit fearful of sincerity. In recent years generally there's been more of an ironic stance and maybe a reluctance to come across as sincere. I don't know. Even the word seems so gauche in a way. On the other hand, sincerity in books can be fairly icky, as if every single thing is meaningful, and no humour at all. I just wrote whatever seemed to matter to me. And that was a revelation. It was really quite exciting, so I just went with it. I didn't have a plan. I didn't really know why I was working on bringing together that particular assortment of pieces, but I felt very strongly that they belonged together. It took me ages to understand the function of each one and how they all related to one another. I wasn't that worried though, because I trust that there's a very good reason why something comes up. It's better not to force things because connections become apparent to me eventually, when I'm a good bit into it.

**AB:** It's odd because in certain ways it feels like a disparate collection of memories or events or thoughts and yet as you make your way through the book, you do feel it hanging together. That said, I've read it three times now and still can't quite identify what that thing is. It's almost like it's not one thing but a series of inter-dependencies between the different episodes and the different concerns such as class, or writing, or womanhood. They work in an equilibrium with each other.

**CLB:** I think I create a sort of connective tissue on a very intricate kind of level. I love when I've pretty much got all the pieces together – I know what's there, and why. Then I need to work on how they sit with each other. That part is almost like sculpting. I'm really going into it with a little toolkit. It's like engineering or something. There'll be small motifs or qualities that I can bring out and create links with or riff on. Like the idea of hot and cold that runs throughout it and is referenced in various different ways. If you're working on that level, it's almost like you're underground in the basement, tinkering with the foundations and the pipe-work. That's what's going to give it an overall sense of cohesiveness.

**AB:** That comes across in the Tarquin Superbus section where you are essentially revisiting a story that was written many years previously, although without any direct access to the original. It's fascinating as a reader to see what a writer would make of a story they remembered, or half-remembered, from an earlier stage.

**CLB:** That was a funny section because I had envisaged that it would maybe be a couple of paragraphs long. I wasn't sure what I was doing when I embarked upon that particular piece. Many years ago I wrote a story about a wealthy man. People will know from my first book that I'm not a character- or plot-orientated writer. So this is a rare thing actually. Once upon a time I did write, or begin to write, a story about a character with a strange name. As it went along his character changed. My characterisation was a bit unstable, a bit uncertain. To begin with he seemed like a stereo-typical European, nineteenth-century kind of chap. But then of course with the rewriting years later I was more confident and the character became richer. You know, you often hear authors talking about characters coming to life, and I've never really had that experience. So it was interesting to spend time with that. And I wanted that development to be apparent to the reader, so each of the characters are quite two-dimensional to begin with, like stock characters from old tales, and then bit by bit they become fuller, more human I suppose. More tender anyway, though that might be more to do with my feelings towards them. I think it's probably as well that I don't invent characters very often – I'd feel enormously protective towards them, it would be awful.

**AB:** A lot of times during this conversation I've mentioned things that I could identify with. But there's one strand of the book which, for relatively obvious reasons, was quite alien to me: the experience of womanhood, of being a teenage girl, becoming a woman, of being a woman who writes, and the kind of reaction that sometimes provokes in certain men with whom you may be in a relationship, for example. I remember talking about *Checkout 19* with colleagues who'd also read it and the women all immediately identified the frankness and the accuracy with which you talk about having your period at school, and the description of the blood and how the colour was so perfect that you wanted to take it to a makeup counter and ask for lipstick in this particular shade.

**CLB:** I was thinking about the fact that I won't go on having periods forever. I quite like them for some reason. For years I used tampons, and then I didn't want to any more. That was quite funny because I couldn't remember ever deciding to use tampons. You just did it and that was that. I got curious about that because it seems like such an important, intimate decision, about how you're treating your body and how you're thinking about what's happening with your body month after month, year after year. It's like trying to minimise this occurrence and make it invisible, and I wanted the visibility of it. I wanted it to be more apparent that I was having my period. Many people of our age remember those Bodyform adverts, like your life doesn't have to stop, you can carry on playing frisbee and riding horses. Maybe you just don't want to, you know. Maybe you just don't flipping feel like it! It's a real shame, all that upbeat nonsense, because your menstrual cycle is really, really interesting and if you tune into its ebbs and flows it can be really helpful. If you're pretending it's not there, and if you think it's going to disappear just by putting a tampon in, that's dumb. That's just not how it works. All the hormones are not going to stop just because you can't see the blood any more. It's a very weird way of treating it. Once it started to become more visible, I started to notice stuff like, 'Oh wow I bled a lot these last few hours, what's going on?' Or I'd notice the colour changing and so on, and all this is actually a really important part of our experience. I don't particularly want to make a big thing out of it, I just do remember leaking at school and that's another part of being a female.

# Geoff Dyer

## *The Last Days of Roger Federer and Other Endings*

### Monday 11 July 2022

~

**Adam Biles:** There are few people who can write so brilliantly about so many things all at once as today's guest, and his new book *The Last Days of Roger Federer and Other Endings* could be his most wide-ranging to date. It's about tennis, specifically about the curtain dropping on the career of one of the most successful and technically beautiful players ever. But it's also about endings of so many other kinds, the significance or otherwise of an artist's last work, mental and intellectual decline, finishing and not finishing books. That writer could only be Geoff Dyer. Geoff, welcome to Shakespeare and Company.

**Geoff Dyer:** Oh, thank you Adam. So happy to be back here.

**AB:** And the day after Novak Djokovic won his seventh Wimbledon title.

**GD:** Right!

**AB:** So before we delve into the book, did you watch the match?

**GD:** I arrived in Paris yesterday and was able to start watching from the third set in my hotel. The strange thing was that I wanted neither of them to win. Kyrgios is great fun to watch as a tennis player, but I found his match against Tsitsipas so distasteful. Even yesterday, when his behaviour by his standards was reasonable, it was still entirely unacceptable. Although one has issues with Djokovic for other reasons, when he's on court he's actually quite gracious. So it was probably a happy outcome.

**AB:** You don't actually spend that much time writing specifically about Roger Federer in the book, but he definitely looms over it. Could you talk about what for you sets him apart. On paper he's not the greatest tennis player ever. So what distinguishes him from the rest of the so-called big four?

**GD:** I wish I had something original to say about Roger. I'd always loved watching him. About five years ago I realised I loved him more than ever! I think that was quite a common feeling because there was a phase when we were taking his greatness for granted. Then he started losing. The remarkable thing was that even when this seemed to be an unbreakable pattern he brushed aside all questions about whether he should pack it in. He didn't consider retiring because what he loved was playing tennis, even if he wasn't winning titles. More importantly, he loved every aspect of being on the tour.

Then there was this remarkable thing whereby, after he seemed to have accepted that he was only ever going to be the runner-up, he came back from surgery and promptly won the Australian Open, Indian Wells, Miami and Wimbledon. What that final blaze of glory at the end of the day reaffirmed was something that we had taken for granted: that the most efficient way of playing tennis, with winning as an indicator of efficiency, could also be the most aesthetically pleasing. That coming together of results plus aesthetic pleasure is very rare in sport. And it combined with something else. What do we look for in sport? Glory, excellence but also, importantly, sportsmanship. The way he'd had to learn to become a gracious loser before he became a winner again – all of these things meant that we had a more intense appreciation of what he'd done.

**AB:** You also say that it was during an Andy Murray press conference – in which he announced what amounted to his retirement – that you decided to write a book about endings. Beyond Roger and Andy, what was it about this moment in history, and this moment in your life, that made you want to take on this subject now?

**GD:** I'd been thinking about writing a book about last things for a while. It's useful to make a slight distinction here. So much work has been done on late style. This is a fairly well-trodden area of academic interest. Beethoven is the classic case because his last works were his late works. But it's not always the case and we can think of examples of last works which really come in the middle phase of an artist's life. If Beethoven happened to have dropped dead however many years previously, his last works would have coincided with what we now regard as his middle phase. In the book I talk about Coltrane. Coltrane dies in his forties. Those last works of Coltrane's are so clearly transitional works, in which he's trying to work out what to do next. He hadn't got near his late phase, it seems to me. And we can think of all sorts of writers whose *first* book turns out to be their last.

One of the questions you ask when embarking on a book is: is it the right time? Then along comes Andy Murray and that press conference when he said 'this is pretty much it for me'. That served to concentrate my mind. There always comes a time when you have to commit yourself pretty much exclusively to writing a book – and this was that moment.

Then during the time I was writing it, the world as we knew it actually came to an end. Which provided a nice larger structure of feeling to encompass these various studies of individual people. I was at a phase of my life when I became conscious that I wasn't thirty any more. I don't feel I'm at death's door and I don't feel my brain is about to pack in. But I felt this was a good time to address these concerns.

**AB:** That's an interesting distinction between sportspeople and artists. With Andy Murray, it was clear because of his injuries that this part of his life as an elite sportsman was going to come to an end. Whereas with writers and artists it's not quite so marked.

**GD:** Exactly. With athletes, of course, it happens in public. But in a way they do share a similar trajectory with artists. You're full of youthful promise. If things go well, you'll achieve some sort of peak. Then there's the decline. In tennis players you can judge that. You can see that by the weekly falling in rankings. It's more subtle with the writer, but there tends to be a falling-off at an uncertain point.

The interesting thing about the writing life, apart from the fact that it can extend into your seventies or eighties, is that sometimes a condition of one's being able to enjoy this creative longevity is that you're necessarily oblivious to what is clear to your readers. That there *has* been a falling-off in quality. In the book I discuss Martin Amis, who for a male writer of my generation is a godlike figure. For me, *Yellow Dog* and *Lionel Asbo* were so poor. For somebody like Amis who's got such a highly evolved sensibility as a reader, you wonder, could he not see what was so obvious to us? When I read *Inside Story*, I was so happy to find such an improvement in quality and depth there. Having said that, you go back to some of the earlier books when he was really on fire and you realise it's not got quite the same force.

**AB:** You write that the value of a life cannot be assessed chrono-logically, which really struck me as something we don't allow to . . . well, to anybody to be honest, but particularly to writers and artists. You write about Kerouac that from the time he completed *On the Road* he was indemnified against ever making or ever having made a serious mistake in his life. I'm curious about why you think we expect each of their successive works to meet the heights of the previous ones. And if they don't, we often treat the previous works as if they were in some way sullied.

**GD:** We have some inbuilt ameliorative urge whereby we want things to get better over time. The other thing that we have this fondness for is the idea that while maybe there's a physical or technical deterioration, that can actually be a component of an overall gain in quality. I know it's bad form to quote Bono, but I remember something he said about Pavarotti. Pavarotti was touring like mad. Everybody wanted to see him. And the voice wasn't what it was like before. A lot of people were critical of this. But Bono said 'what are these people talking about?'. All sorts of things can mean that the voice could, in spite of the decline, somehow be better than ever. It's even more marked with Callas, the ultimate tragic diva. How important is it that she was no longer capable of reaching whatever note it is? Isn't her inability to do that going to enhance the tragic quality of the roles she's playing?

Kerouac is such an important figure to me. The typical position regarding *On the Road* is you read it when you're eighteen, nineteen, twenty and it's great, and then you read it when you're twenty-eight and you think, 'Hmm, I've grown out of this.' I've never grown out of it. Every time I reread it, it seems to me more profound. The fact that he became this rather buffoonish, alcoholic mess really doesn't count for anything in the face of that great achievement. At some level he was conscious of that, and that's why he was willing to let himself go and just become this pudgy drunk living with his mum.

**AB:** A lot of Kerouac's later works are dismissed as lesser works, but I do think there's something interesting there, and in his earlier works, which is often underplayed. And that's the blue collar confrontation with fluid sexuality. I'm waiting for somebody to resurrect Kerouac as a kind of early exponent of blue-collar homosexuality or bisexuality.

I'd like to pick up on that idea of the blue-collar nature of Kerouac. You say that retirement in the world you grew up in – the world of poorly paid and unpleasant and unrewarding work – was something your relatives began to look forward to from a surprisingly early age. I have exactly the same thing. My father retired maybe ten years ago now. Being in the world of books, where people don't admit to either a desire to retire or even that retirement is possible, I remember thinking, 'Oh, gosh, what's he going to do with his time?' But I was struck by how much he embraced retirement after a long period of physically and mentally demanding work. Do you think there's a class dimension to this desire of wanting things to be over with?

**GD:** The immediate response is yes, in terms of work. I've had so little experience of working at a regular job. But when you do have a regular job, you're aware of how much it's eating into your time, and therefore you long for the weekends and you get this sense of dread when once again your life is going to be taken away from you on a Monday morning. If we change the framework from days of the week into years of the life, then of course you look forward to no longer having to do this thing as a way of earning money and just being able to give yourself entirely to life. But in the writer's life, there's no difference at all between work and leisure. All you're doing is living your life. So, with regard to retirement, there's not going to be this moment when suddenly you're not going into the place of work any more. What there might be instead is a gradual diminution of productivity, but you'll be spending your time ostensibly in the same way. You'll certainly be reading a lot. This in turn leads to one of the other major concerns of the book.

I'm so hostile to those books – and you've probably got a load of them downstairs – where the cover copy announces the scenario of 'an afternoon that will change the characters' lives forever'. Of course, it is possible I could step outside, get hit by a truck and spend the rest of my life in a wheelchair, and yeah, that would change my life forever. But more commonly, it's the way that one's life changes *gradually* that is remarkable. Authorial retirement is very much a gradual alteration.

**AB:** You write about going to poetry readings or concerts, and how there's always a part of you longing for it to be finished. I identified with that completely. But I immediately thought of a friend who I was sure would feel differently. So I wrote to him about it and he said, 'Yes, absolutely. I feel that too.'

**GD:** One sometimes finds oneself saying about a book by Dickens, *Little Dorrit* or whatever: I never wanted it to end. It's sort of true, except as you're going through it you're also thinking, 'Oh, great, page 500. I've broken the back of it. Phew!' There's always that sense of relief to have got to the end.

And there are so many manifestations of this. Like when you're on your way home from a trip, you get off the plane and then of course you want to be first off, and there's that rush to get to passport control. Every person you overtake, especially in America, you're going to gain ten minutes. Sometimes it goes well and sometimes it doesn't. Then typically you get home and you're in this weird, 'Oh, what do I do now?' You just sit there. It's like a little parable. Just speeding through it was the purpose and what you're actually going to do now with this time you've saved is beside the point.

**AB:** You talk about giving up on books with what feels like a gleeful abandon. You list this roster of classics – *The Brothers Karamazov, The Man Without Qualities, Finnegans Wake* – which you seem to take delight in not having finished.

**GD:** Well, I derive no satisfaction from not having finished *The Brothers Karamazov*. I wish I had done, although I should have finished it when I was twenty or something when I had the stamina. I really don't want to go to my grave without having read Proust properly. But actually I seem to make less and less progress with Proust every time I try. So it's not so much gleeful as just being honest, really.

The other thing is the opportunity cost of persisting with a given book when you think, 'If I read this then I'm not going to get on to that', although this is in keeping with that earlier parable about hurrying through immigration to get home. Quite often I'll abandon a book in the name of devoting that time to something else. And then what do I do with that time? I don't read anything! I just sit there, stunned. There are many different versions of this, but all of them, I think, are quite widely shared.

**AB:** I'd like to come back to this idea of the artist's last work. As you alluded to earlier, there are different 'lasts'. There is the work that somebody creates after a slow decline at a very old age. There's also somebody who dies suddenly. Either way there is a certain glamour associated with the last. What do you think underlies that?

**GD:** Some basic teleological concern. There might be exceptions, but for the moment, let's say that Beethoven is the apotheosis of this. There's early Beethoven, there's mid Beethoven, by which time he's the greatest composer in the world. And then there's late Beethoven, where it's pretty much beyond people's capacity to appreciate what he's doing or even play what's he's written. This is inextricably linked to his deafness. He's doing really far-out stuff at the end of his life. And of course stuff has come out since that is even more far-out, but it couldn't have existed without Beethoven. A person of such genius, and in particular historical circumstances, can burst out of time. So: how and *when* does it happen, this bursting out of time?

**AB:** Which brings us nicely on to Nietzsche.

**GD:** You were taking a while to get around to him.

**AB:** He is quite a thread through the book.

**GD:** I think he's the single most important figure in the book.

**AB:** When I studied Nietzsche first at the age of seventeen, eighteen and then again at university, I felt that he was repeatedly sold as a young man's philosopher. The philosopher that you might grow out of at some point and move on to more serious things. And yet, after revisiting him in recent years, I actually came to think (and your book confirmed this for me) that the reverse is true. There's so much about Nietzsche, which is about stripping away the carapace life has built around you that, as a young man, one is almost incapable of identifying with the radical nature in his writing.

**GD:** There's a joke I make in the book that because I have no training in philosophy, I took to Nietzsche like a duck to water. Most philosophy I can't understand. But we could pick up a volume of Nietzsche and turn to a page at random, and there'd be some lightning flash of illumination. When I was about nineteen, after I first read *Middlemarch*, I understood so much about relationships, gestures, morality, that was way in excess of my life experience. When I reread it recently in my sixties, I experienced again what

I had learnt from it, as it were. Similarly with Nietzsche, you read it when you're young and there are these great shockwaves. But the subtlety and nuance of his novelistic, psychological understanding of things is also incredible – and you're getting it without the 900 pages of other stuff that's going on in *Middlemarch*.

**AB:** There's something interesting about approaching it as literature. A distinct feeling I had after reading him was that the separation between philosophy and literature had been broken. As if the philosophers were perhaps masquerading as people dealing in truth, in a way that novelists didn't necessarily pretend to. Nietzsche's writing blurred that because it's so clearly literature, but in the guise of philosophy.

**GD:** Nietzsche was keen on calling himself a psychologist. This is remarkable, especially since he's describing a branch of psychology which is in the process of formation – but which had been developing in another form in the novel – that is to say the post-Christian or post-religious psychology.

And Nietzsche's life is so poignant, really. His stunning lack of success. Just wandering from place to place in Europe with only news of an occasional reader somewhere to cheer him up. Eventually the scale of the neglect is such that he falls prey to the familiar solace of rampant megalomania: exactly the kind of condition he was so astute at describing and analysing.

**AB:** Ironically, and tragically, what brought him to prominence was a corruption of his work by his sister.

**GD:** Yes, indeed. Although I like a humanist version of Nietzsche. There is a Nietzsche for everyone; we can find the proto-fascist Nietzsche if we utilise that blunt instrument John Carey as a guide. We could also find the feminist Nietzsche, which is quite something given that famous line about when you go to see your woman, don't forget your whip. There's a Nietzsche for everybody if one looks hard enough and quotes selectively.

**AB:** And of course, he was a writer who had difficulty ending the books he was working on. *The Gay Science* has a prologue of verse and an appendix of song or something like that?

**GD:** Preludes, prologues, the text itself – and then the afterwords, epilogues, postscripts! Once he gets to Wagner, there's really no end to it. Pretty much the last thing he does is compile that anthology from his previous work to show that even when he was most infatuated with Wagner he was already turning against him.

**AB:** The idea which he considered his most important and the last thing we're going to talk about today is eternal recurrence.

**GD:** You're absolutely right. This is what he considered his key idea. Which is that this life as you now lead it, you will live over and over again throughout eternity. It's his most emphatic and complete rejection of Christian salvation. Seventy years of suffering? That's nothing compared with an eternity of bliss. Whereas with this idea of his you've got only *this* life: there's no escape from it.

**AB:** And you will live it again and again and again and again . . .

**GD:** And again! When he first quietly announces this in *The Gay Science*, he says (to paraphrase), 'if somebody told you this in your loneliest loneliness, wouldn't you clutch your head and say, "this is just terrible"?' Then he says, 'Has there ever been a moment in your life when you'd say, "You're a God? I've never heard anything more divine."' We think of moments of heartbreak or boredom that are awful. But then there are moments when you first fall in love, or in my case, when I saw that I'd got my three grade A A-levels. I'd happily live that morning again when that letter came in the post! But, as he says, you can't pick and choose. You can't say, 'Oh, yeah, I'll have the greatest hits, but I won't have all the drudgery.' That ends up linking back to tennis because we think of poor old Boris Becker now, a ludicrous figure. Where is he now? He's banged up somewhere in jail. This is a phase of his life he's probably not keen to live over and over again. But remember what Nietzsche adds: 'but have you ever known a moment?' So you think of how at nineteen or whatever it was, Becker wins Wimbledon, raises his arms in victory. What a great moment. Is that going to be enough to sustain him through all eternity? I say that because it's so far beyond anything any of us will ever experience. It's another way of affirming that a life can't be assessed chronologically because right now my life is loads better than Boris Becker's. His life sucks in comparison with mine. But what's the distance between the high point in my life, which we'll say was those three grade A A-levels, and his winning Wimbledon at approximately the same age? It's colossal.

**AB:** This is an unfair question to finish on: do you find solace in the fact that perhaps your life has been on more of a level than Boris Becker's . . . ?

**GD:** You mean, I've just plodded along like a hamster? No, wait. A hamster goes round and round . . .

**AB:** But if you could choose between, a life of small troughs, but also small peaks, or vast peaks, but equally vast troughs . . .

**GD:** Nietzsche urges us to choose: how we're going to live *now*. It so happens that as I walked here today past Notre Dame, which is being restored, I was listening to 'Theme de Yoyo' by the Art

Ensemble of Chicago, which was recorded while they were living here in France, in 1970 I think. Anyway, walking and listening to this great track I was conscious of a surge of well-being. I was in Paris, the weather was lovely, I was on my way to meet you to blah on about my books – and it was wonderful. And I wouldn't have known about the Art Ensemble were it not for my friend Chris Mitchell who I met at Oxford in about 1978. So while it might seem that I'm dodging your question where you rather ruthlessly asked if I would prefer to be me or Boris Becker, I don't think I am because this is a day I'll look forward to living over and over. Actually, I need to add another word or two about Notre Dame, both the original building and the current project of reconstruction. Writers talk about how hard it is to write a book, but actually it's quite easy. You just sit there for a year or so. But how do you go about rebuilding a wonder of the world like this? I mean, I'd like to meet the person in charge of that. And when it is rebuilt, it'll be a wonderful achievement that we can all share in, people of all religions and atheists alike. Nietzsche, of course, was hostile to churches but I'm more of the Larkin persuasion: a place like this has an immense power and it played a part in making this day special. So the roots of this day extend beyond the autobiograph-ical; they're historic as well as personal.

# Acknowledgements

~

We'd like to express our gratitude to the following people, without whom this book wouldn't have been possible.

Nicole Aragi, Pippa Barlow, Claire-Louise Bennett, Francis Bickmore, Anne Bielec, Jemma Birrell, Helen Bleck, Ben Brown, Jamie Byng, Charles Buchan, Kit Caless, Clare Conville, Rachel Cusk, Lorenza Dalloca, Geoff Dyer, Reni Eddo-Lodge, Ros Ellis, Annie Ernaux, Percival Everett, Linda Fallon, John Freeman, Alex Freiman, Francis Geffard, Helena Gonda, Audrey Gouimenou, Neil Gower, David Grove, Krista Halverson, Aa'Ishah Hawton, Alice Heathwood, Aisling Holling, Octavia Horgan, Marlon James, Meena Kandasamy, Laura Keeling, Katie Kitamura, Karl Ove Knausgaard, Hari Kunzru, Deborah Landau, Ellen Levine, Olivia Laing, David McKeary, Madeleine Miller, Margot Miriel, Jamie Norman, Juliette Ponce, Simon Prosser, Claire Reiderman, Carlo Rovelli, Vicki Rutherford, George Saunders, Steph Scott, Leïla Slimani, Miles Temel, Miriam Toews, Edward Wall, Jesmyn Ward, Sarah Watling, Colson Whitehead, Jenny Zhang . . . and all the Shakespeare and Company booksellers and Tumbleweeds who helped set up and run the events in the book.

# Permission Credits

~

# Permission Credits

Interview with Hari Kunzru, Copyright © Hari Kunzru. Reprinted by permission of Hari Kunzru.

Interview with Leïla Slimani, Copyright © Leïla Slimani. Reprinted by permission of Leïla Slimani.

Interview with Jesmyn Ward, Copyright © Jesmyn Ward. Reprinted by permission of Jesmyn Ward.

Interview with Reni Eddo-Lodge, Copyright © Reni Eddo-Lodge. Reprinted by permission of Reni Eddo-Lodge.

Interview with Carlo Rovelli, Copyright © Carlo Rovelli. Reprinted by permission of Carlo Rovelli.

Interview with Jenny Zhang, Copyright © Jenny Zhang. Reprinted by permission of Jenny Zhang.

Interview with Annie Ernaux, Copyright © Annie Ernaux. Reprinted by permission of Annie Ernaux.

Interview with Rachel Cusk, Copyright © Rachel Cusk. Reprinted by permission of Rachel Cusk.

Interview with Meena Kandasamy, Copyright © Meena Kandasamy. Reprinted by permission of Meena Kandasamy.

Interview with Madeline Miller, Copyright © Madeline Miller. Reprinted by permission of Madeline Miller.

Interview with Miriam Toews, Copyright © Miriam Toews. Reprinted by permission of Miriam Toews.